# Literacy Launch

## TEACHER'S PLANNING GUIDE

**Macmillan**
**McGraw-Hill**

NEW YORK     FARMINGTON

# Literary Launch

# Contents

Philosophy . . . . . . . . . . . . . . . . . . . . . . . . . . . . . . . . . . . . . . . . . .iv-v
How to Use the Book . . . . . . . . . . . . . . . . . . . . . . . . . . . . . . . . . .vi
Prebook Activities . . . . . . . . . . . . . . . . . . . . . . . . . . . . . . . . . . . .vii

**Lesson 1**   Listening, Speaking, Viewing  . . . . . . . . . . . . . . . .5-5a
**Lesson 2**   Listening, Speaking, Viewing . . . . . . . . . . . . . . . . .6-6a
**Lesson 3**   Letter Identification: *B, C, T, N, A* . . . . . . . . . . . . . .7-7a
**Lesson 4**   Letter Identification: *b, c, t, n, a* . . . . . . . . . . . . . . .8-8a
**Lesson 5**   Auditory Discrimination: /b/*b* . . . . . . . . . . . . . . . .9-9a
**Lesson 6**   Initial Consonant: /b/*b* . . . . . . . . . . . . . . . . . . . . .10-10a
**Lesson 7**   Auditory Discrimination: /k/*c* . . . . . . . . . . . . . . . .11-11a
**Lesson 8**   Initial Consonant: /k/*c* . . . . . . . . . . . . . . . . . . . . .12-12a
**Lesson 9**   Auditory Discrimination: /t/*t* . . . . . . . . . . . . . . . .13-13a
**Lesson 10**  Initial Consonant: /t/*t* . . . . . . . . . . . . . . . . . . . . .14-14a
**Lesson 11**  Auditory Discrimination: /n/*n* . . . . . . . . . . . . . . .15-15a
**Lesson 12**  Initial Consonant: /n/*n* . . . . . . . . . . . . . . . . . . . .16-16a
**Lesson 13**  Auditory Discrimination: /a/*a* . . . . . . . . . . . . . . .17-17a
**Lesson 14**  Initial Vowel: /a/*a* . . . . . . . . . . . . . . . . . . . . . . . .18-18a

**Lesson 15 • Review**  Initial Consonants Review:
/b/*b*, /k/*c*, /t/*t*, /n/*n* . . . . . . . . . . . . . . . . . . . . . . . . . . . . . .19-19a

**Lesson 16**  Listening, Speaking, Viewing  . . . . . . . . . . . . . . .20-20a
**Lesson 17**  Letter Identification: *D, F, G, H, E* . . . . . . . . . . . . .21-21a
**Lesson 18**  Letter Identification: *d, f, g, h, e* . . . . . . . . . . . . . .22-22a
**Lesson 19**  Auditory Discrimination: /d/*d* . . . . . . . . . . . . . . .23-23a
**Lesson 20**  Initial Consonant: /d/*d* . . . . . . . . . . . . . . . . . . . .24-24a
**Lesson 21**  Auditory Discrimination:/f/*f* . . . . . . . . . . . . . . . .25-25a
**Lesson 22**  Initial Consonant: /f/*f* . . . . . . . . . . . . . . . . . . . . .26-26a
**Lesson 23**  Auditory Discrimination: /g/*g* . . . . . . . . . . . . . . .27-27a
**Lesson 24**  Initial Consonant: /g/*g*. . . . . . . . . . . . . . . . . . . . .28-28a
**Lesson 25**  Auditory Discrimination: /h/*b* . . . . . . . . . . . . . . .29-29a
**Lesson 26**  Initial Consonant: /h/*b*. . . . . . . . . . . . . . . . . . . . .30-30a
**Lesson 27**  Auditory Discrimination: /e/*e* . . . . . . . . . . . . . . .31-31a
**Lesson 28**  Initial Vowel: /e/*e* . . . . . . . . . . . . . . . . . . . . . . . .32-32a

**Lesson 29 • Review**  Initial Consonants Review:
/d/*d*, /f/*f*, /g/*g*, /h/*b* . . . . . . . . . . . . . . . . . . . . . . . . . . . . . .33-33a

**Lesson 30**  Listening, Speaking, Viewing  . . . . . . . . . . . . . . .34-34a
**Lesson 31**  Letter Identification: *J, M, P, L, O* . . . . . . . . . . . . .35-35a
**Lesson 32**  Letter Identification: *j, m, p, l, o* . . . . . . . . . . . . . .36-36a
**Lesson 33**  Auditory Discrimination: /j/*j* . . . . . . . . . . . . . . . .37-37a
**Lesson 34**  Initial Consonant: /j/*j* . . . . . . . . . . . . . . . . . . . . .38-38a
**Lesson 35**  Auditory Discrimination: /m/*m* . . . . . . . . . . . . . .39-39a

**Lesson 36**    Initial Consonant: /m/*m* . . . . . . . . . . . . . . . . . . . . . . . . . . .40-40a
**Lesson 37**    Auditory Discrimination: /p/*p* . . . . . . . . . . . . . . . . . . . . . . .41-41a
**Lesson 38**    Initial Consonant: /p/*p* . . . . . . . . . . . . . . . . . . . . . . . . . . . .42-42a
**Lesson 39**    Auditory Discrimination: /l/*l* . . . . . . . . . . . . . . . . . . . . . . .43-43a
**Lesson 40**    Initial Consonant: /l/*l* . . . . . . . . . . . . . . . . . . . . . . . . . . . . .44-44a
**Lesson 41**    Auditory Discrimination: /o/*o*. . . . . . . . . . . . . . . . . . . . . . .45-45a
**Lesson 42**    Initial Vowel: /o/*o* . . . . . . . . . . . . . . . . . . . . . . . . . . . . . . . .46-46a

**Lesson 43 • Review**  Initial Consonants Review:
/j/*j*, /m/*m*, /p/*p*, /l/*l* . . . . . . . . . . . . . . . . . . . . . . . . . . . .47-47a

**Lesson 44**    Listening, Speaking, Viewing  . . . . . . . . . . . . . . . . . . . . . . .48-48a
**Lesson 45**    Letter Identification: *K, R, S, V, I* . . . . . . . . . . . . . . . . . . . .49-49a
**Lesson 46**    Letter Identification: *k, r, s, v, i* . . . . . . . . . . . . . . . . . . . . .50-50a
**Lesson 47**    Auditory Discrimination: /k/*k* . . . . . . . . . . . . . . . . . . . . . . .51-51a
**Lesson 48**    Initial Consonant: /k/*k* . . . . . . . . . . . . . . . . . . . . . . . . . . . .52-52a
**Lesson 49**    Auditory Discrimination: /r/*r* . . . . . . . . . . . . . . . . . . . . . . .53-53a
**Lesson 50**    Initial  Consonant: /r/*r* . . . . . . . . . . . . . . . . . . . . . . . . . . . .54-54a
**Lesson 51**    Auditory Discrimination: /s/*s* . . . . . . . . . . . . . . . . . . . . . . .55-55a
**Lesson 52**    Initial Consonant: /s/*s* . . . . . . . . . . . . . . . . . . . . . . . . . . . .56-56a
**Lesson 53**    Auditory Discrimination: /v/*v* . . . . . . . . . . . . . . . . . . . . . . .57-57a
**Lesson 54**    Initial  Consonant: /v/*v* . . . . . . . . . . . . . . . . . . . . . . . . . . . .58-58a
**Lesson 55**    Auditory Discrimination: /i/*i* . . . . . . . . . . . . . . . . . . . . . . . .59-59a
**Lesson 56**    Initial Vowel: /i/*i* . . . . . . . . . . . . . . . . . . . . . . . . . . . . . . . . .60-60a

**Lesson 57 • Review**  Initial Consonants Review:
/k/*k*, /r/r, /s/*s*, /v/*v* . . . . . . . . . . . . . . . . . . . . . . . . . . . . .61-61a

**Lesson 58**    Listening, Speaking, Viewing  . . . . . . . . . . . . . . . . . . . . . . .62-62a
**Lesson 59**    Letter Identification: *Q, W, Y, Z, U* . . . . . . . . . . . . . . . . . . .63-63a
**Lesson 60**    Letter Identification: *q, w, y, z, u* . . . . . . . . . . . . . . . . . . . .64-64a
**Lesson 61**    Auditory Discrimination: /kw/*qu* . . . . . . . . . . . . . . . . . . . .65-65a
**Lesson 62**    Initial Consonant: /kw/*qu* . . . . . . . . . . . . . . . . . . . . . . . . .66-66a
**Lesson 63**    Auditory Discrimination: /w/*w* . . . . . . . . . . . . . . . . . . . . . .67-67a
**Lesson 64**    Initial  Consonant: /w/*w* . . . . . . . . . . . . . . . . . . . . . . . . . .68-68a
**Lesson 65**    Auditory Discrimination: /y/*y* . . . . . . . . . . . . . . . . . . . . . . .69-69a
**Lesson 66**    Initial Consonant: /y/*y* . . . . . . . . . . . . . . . . . . . . . . . . . . . .70-70a
**Lesson 67**    Auditory Discrimination: /z/*z* . . . . . . . . . . . . . . . . . . . . . . .71-71a
**Lesson 68**    Initial  Consonant: /z/*z* . . . . . . . . . . . . . . . . . . . . . . . . . . . .72-72a
**Lesson 69**    Auditory Discrimination: /u/*u* . . . . . . . . . . . . . . . . . . . . . . .73-73a
**Lesson 70**    Initial Vowel: /u/*u* . . . . . . . . . . . . . . . . . . . . . . . . . . . . . . .74-74a

**Lesson 71 • Review**  Initial Consonants Review:
/kw/*qu*, /w/*w*, /y/*y*, /z/*z* . . . . . . . . . . . . . . . . . . . . . . . . .75-75a

**Picture Cards** . . . . . . . . . . . . . . . . . . . . . . . . . . . . . . . . . . . . . . . . . .76-82

# Philosophy

## SPOTLIGHT ON LITERACY

***Spotlight on Literacy*** recognizes that children come from many different backgrounds and bring with them various experiences. All children are emerging readers and writers who have valuable input to offer to the class. It is an important goal of the teacher to evaluate each child's strengths and weaknesses and provide the individualized support that will help him or her move into conventional reading and writing.

## LITERACY LAUNCH

*Literacy Launch* is one of the many ways in which ***Spotlight on Literacy*** offers the support needed to address children's individual needs. As children enter first grade, you will find that some of them have a firm understanding of basic skills and concepts such as letter identification, auditory discrimination, and letter formation. However, there may also be children who have not had much exposure to literature prior to entering school. Therefore they may need instruction for these skills and concepts to aid in their development into independent readers. The activities offered in this book address the following basic skills and concepts: listening, speaking, viewing, letter identification, auditory discrimination, initial consonants and short vowels.

## LISTENING, SPEAKING, VIEWING

Children begin with a Shared Book experience using *Zoo-Be-Doo* by Beth Alley Wise. Opportunities for developing listening, speaking, and viewing skills abound as children listen to the Big Book being read aloud, and personally respond to the story. Later, the children may use the Little Books to reread the story independently or in pairs.

Subsequent lessons offer additional opportunities for developing listening, speaking, and viewing skills as well as reinforcing such comprehension skills as recalling details, forming categories, and sequencing events.

## LETTER IDENTIFICATION

Children identify upper- and lowercase letters of the alphabet. Shapes and colors are also reinforced as children use visual cues to complete each page.

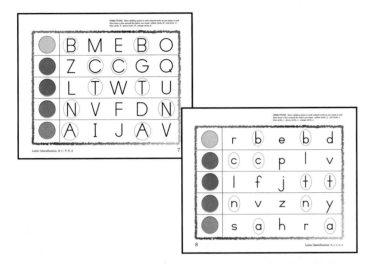

## INITIAL CONSONANTS & SHORT VOWELS

Children make connections between initial consonant sounds, initial short vowels, and the letters that represent those sounds. In addition, letter formation is reinforced.

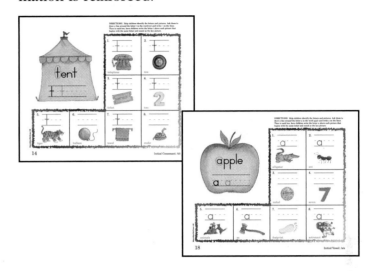

## AUDITORY DISCRIMINATION

Letter sounds are taught to help children discriminate among initial sounds.

## REVIEW

Five review lessons are provided to offer reinforcement for the skills taught. These pages can also serve as assessment opportunities.

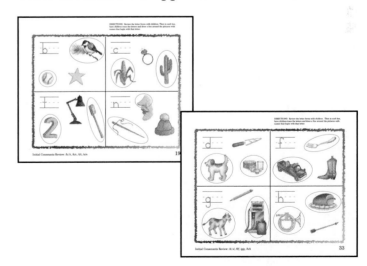

# How to Use the Book

*Literacy Launch* is designed so that you can pick and choose the lessons that you think will best address the specific needs of each child in your class. Use it during the first three or four weeks of the school year to help reinforce the basic skills that children need as they grow into independent readers. *Literacy Launch* is divided into five sections. Each section focuses on four consonants and a short vowel. After a lesson devoted to listening, speaking, and viewing activities, children learn to identify the upper- and lowercase letters. Then, separate lessons on auditory discrimination and the letter/sound connection are taught for each of the five letters. Finally, each section concludes with a review lesson to reinforce the skills taught.

Keep in mind that as children work with these pages, it is important for them to continue to enjoy literature experiences by reading and responding to a variety of books and stories each day.

You may wish to use the following suggestions to help determine how best to use *Literacy Launch*.

➡ Use the review pages as a diagnostic tool to determine what concepts and skills children need help with. Then select the appropriate lessons from the table of contents.

➡ Select appropriate lessons that will supplement your teaching of the skills you address with each selection.

➡ For those children who need detailed instruction in letter identification, initial consonants, and activities that reinforce listening, speaking, and viewing skills, use the teaching suggestions offered in this book as children work through each lesson. The review pages can help you assess children's progress.

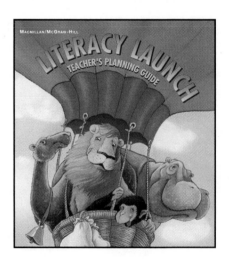

# Prebook Activities

The following Prebook Activities offer a variety of short, concrete learning experiences that can be used with individuals, pairs, or groups. You may wish to use them before starting *Literacy Launch* to help children develop basic skills and concepts, or they may be used to supplement lessons in the book. The activities focus on listening, speaking, and viewing skills, comprehension skills, as well as visual and auditory perception.

## Listening, Speaking, and Viewing Activities

➡ Read a story that extends over a few days. Before each new segment, review what has happened before. Stop at an exciting moment, and ask children what they think might happen next.

➡ Hold a "Discussion Time" with children in which they are encouraged to talk about important experiences in their lives. Be sure to encourage those children who do not often participate in group discussions. Use this time to discuss the day's schedule and special events as well as personal experiences.

➡ Read with children a wordless picture book, such as *The Trunk* by Brian Wildsmith (Oxford University Press, 1982). Encourage children to look at the illustrations and tell the story they see being told through the pictures. Be sure that all children have an opportunity to contribute to the discussion. You might wish to write the children's story as they tell it. Then reread their story with them, using the illustrations in the book.

## Comprehension Activities

➡ To help build children's understanding of sequence of events, discuss familiar stories, television programs, or popular movies with them. Have children tell what happened first, next, and last in each story, episode, or movie. You might also ask children to think about their morning activities and tell, in order, the things that they did.

➡ Provide opportunities for children to sort objects to reinforce the skill of forming categories. Provide objects such as buttons, small-shaped blocks, beads, or rocks. Egg cartons or muffin tins make good sorting trays for these items. Discuss with children the characteristics of the objects that they are sorting.

## Visual Perception Activities

➡ Children can practice identifying different shapes by going on a shape hunt. Display paper squares, triangles, rectangles, and circles. Have children look around the room and find objects that have these shapes.

➡ Have children play a matching game. Make two sets of 3-letter word cards. Invite children to work in small groups and match words that are the same. Remember that children need not know how to read the words in order to match them.

## Auditory Perception Activities

➡ Place a few objects on a table such as a metal spoon, a pin, a book, and a rubber ball. Have children close their eyes. Drop one object and ask children to identify which object was dropped. Repeat the activity with the other objects.

➡ Children can work in groups of four to play a game of "I'm Going on a Trip." The first child can begin by saying *I'm going on a trip and I'm taking my toothbrush.* The second child must repeat the first child's statement and add another item to take on the trip. The game continues as each child repeats the previous statement and adds a new item to take on the trip.

MACMILLAN/McGRAW-HILL

Literacy Launch PRACTICE BOOK

Macmillan
McGraw-Hill
NEW YORK    FARMINGTON

Designed by Michaelis/Carpelis Design Assoc. Inc.
Illustrated by Barbara Epstein-Eagle, Ronda Henrichsen, Pat Hoggan, Gary Holland, Joan
Holob, Loretta Lustig, Deborah Morse, Jeffrey Severn
Cover Illustrated by Michele Noiset

*Macmillan/McGraw-Hill*
A Division of The *McGraw-Hill* Companies

Macmillan/McGraw-Hill
1221 Avenue of the Americas
New York, New York 10020

Printed in the United States of America
ISBN 0-02-181687-5 / 1

1 2 3 4 5 6 7 8 9  WEB  02 01 00 99 98 97

# CONTENTS

Listening, Speaking, Viewing . . . . . . . . . . . . . . . . . . . . . . . . . . . . . . . . . . . . . . . . . . . . . . . . . . . . . . . .5
Listening, Speaking, Viewing . . . . . . . . . . . . . . . . . . . . . . . . . . . . . . . . . . . . . . . . . . . . . . . . . . . . . . . .6
Letter Identification: *B, C, T, N, A* . . . . . . . . . . . . . . . . . . . . . . . . . . . . . . . . . . . . . . . . . . . . . . . . . . . . .7
Letter Identification: *b, c, t, n, a* . . . . . . . . . . . . . . . . . . . . . . . . . . . . . . . . . . . . . . . . . . . . . . . . . . . . .8
Auditory Discrimination: /b/*b* . . . . . . . . . . . . . . . . . . . . . . . . . . . . . . . . . . . . . . . . . . . . . . . . . . . . . . . .9
Initial Consonant: /b/*b* . . . . . . . . . . . . . . . . . . . . . . . . . . . . . . . . . . . . . . . . . . . . . . . . . . . . . . . . . . . .10
Auditory Discrimination: /k/*c* . . . . . . . . . . . . . . . . . . . . . . . . . . . . . . . . . . . . . . . . . . . . . . . . . . . . . . .11
Initial Consonant: /k/*c* . . . . . . . . . . . . . . . . . . . . . . . . . . . . . . . . . . . . . . . . . . . . . . . . . . . . . . . . . . .12
Auditory Discrimination: /t/*t* . . . . . . . . . . . . . . . . . . . . . . . . . . . . . . . . . . . . . . . . . . . . . . . . . . . . . . . .13
Initial Consonant: /t/*t* . . . . . . . . . . . . . . . . . . . . . . . . . . . . . . . . . . . . . . . . . . . . . . . . . . . . . . . . . . . .14
Auditory Discrimination: /n/*n* . . . . . . . . . . . . . . . . . . . . . . . . . . . . . . . . . . . . . . . . . . . . . . . . . . . . . . .15
Initial Consonant: /n/*n* . . . . . . . . . . . . . . . . . . . . . . . . . . . . . . . . . . . . . . . . . . . . . . . . . . . . . . . . . . .16
Auditory Discrimination: /a/*a* . . . . . . . . . . . . . . . . . . . . . . . . . . . . . . . . . . . . . . . . . . . . . . . . . . . . . . .17
Initial Vowel: /a/*a* . . . . . . . . . . . . . . . . . . . . . . . . . . . . . . . . . . . . . . . . . . . . . . . . . . . . . . . . . . . . . . .18
Initial Consonants Review: /b/*b*, /k/*c*, /t/*t*, /n/*n* . . . . . . . . . . . . . . . . . . . . . . . . . . . . . . . . . . . . . .19
Listening, Speaking, Viewing . . . . . . . . . . . . . . . . . . . . . . . . . . . . . . . . . . . . . . . . . . . . . . . . . . . . . . . .20
Letter Identification: *D, F, G, H, E* . . . . . . . . . . . . . . . . . . . . . . . . . . . . . . . . . . . . . . . . . . . . . . . . . . .21
Letter Identification: *d, f, g, h, e* . . . . . . . . . . . . . . . . . . . . . . . . . . . . . . . . . . . . . . . . . . . . . . . . . . . .22
Auditory Discrimination: /d/*d* . . . . . . . . . . . . . . . . . . . . . . . . . . . . . . . . . . . . . . . . . . . . . . . . . . . . . . .23
Initial Consonant: /d/*d* . . . . . . . . . . . . . . . . . . . . . . . . . . . . . . . . . . . . . . . . . . . . . . . . . . . . . . . . . . .24
Auditory Discrimination: /f/*f* . . . . . . . . . . . . . . . . . . . . . . . . . . . . . . . . . . . . . . . . . . . . . . . . . . . . . . . .25
Initial Consonant: /f/*f* . . . . . . . . . . . . . . . . . . . . . . . . . . . . . . . . . . . . . . . . . . . . . . . . . . . . . . . . . . . .26
Auditory Discrimination: /g/*g* . . . . . . . . . . . . . . . . . . . . . . . . . . . . . . . . . . . . . . . . . . . . . . . . . . . . . . .27
Initial Consonant: /g/*g* . . . . . . . . . . . . . . . . . . . . . . . . . . . . . . . . . . . . . . . . . . . . . . . . . . . . . . . . . . .28
Auditory Discrimination: /h/*h* . . . . . . . . . . . . . . . . . . . . . . . . . . . . . . . . . . . . . . . . . . . . . . . . . . . . . . .29
Initial Consonant: /h/*h* . . . . . . . . . . . . . . . . . . . . . . . . . . . . . . . . . . . . . . . . . . . . . . . . . . . . . . . . . . .30
Auditory Discrimination: /e/*e* . . . . . . . . . . . . . . . . . . . . . . . . . . . . . . . . . . . . . . . . . . . . . . . . . . . . . . .31
Initial Vowel: /e/*e* . . . . . . . . . . . . . . . . . . . . . . . . . . . . . . . . . . . . . . . . . . . . . . . . . . . . . . . . . . . . . . .32
Initial Consonants Review: /d/*d*, /f/*f*, /g/*g*, /h/*h* . . . . . . . . . . . . . . . . . . . . . . . . . . . . . . . . . . . . . .33
Listening, Speaking, Viewing . . . . . . . . . . . . . . . . . . . . . . . . . . . . . . . . . . . . . . . . . . . . . . . . . . . . . . . .34
Letter Identification: *J, M, P, L, O* . . . . . . . . . . . . . . . . . . . . . . . . . . . . . . . . . . . . . . . . . . . . . . . . . . . .35
Letter Identification: *j, m, p, l, o* . . . . . . . . . . . . . . . . . . . . . . . . . . . . . . . . . . . . . . . . . . . . . . . . . . . .36
Auditory Discrimination: /j/*j* . . . . . . . . . . . . . . . . . . . . . . . . . . . . . . . . . . . . . . . . . . . . . . . . . . . . . . . .37
Initial Consonant: /j/*j* . . . . . . . . . . . . . . . . . . . . . . . . . . . . . . . . . . . . . . . . . . . . . . . . . . . . . . . . . . . .38

Auditory Discrimination: /m/*m* . . . . . . . . . . . . . . . . . . . . . . . . . . . . . . . . . . . . . . . . . . . . . . . . . . . . . . .39
Initial Consonant: /m/*m* . . . . . . . . . . . . . . . . . . . . . . . . . . . . . . . . . . . . . . . . . . . . . . . . . . . . . . . . . . .40
Auditory Discrimination: /p/*p* . . . . . . . . . . . . . . . . . . . . . . . . . . . . . . . . . . . . . . . . . . . . . . . . . . . . . . .41
Initial Consonant: /p/*p* . . . . . . . . . . . . . . . . . . . . . . . . . . . . . . . . . . . . . . . . . . . . . . . . . . . . . . . . . . .42
Auditory Discrimination: /l/*l* . . . . . . . . . . . . . . . . . . . . . . . . . . . . . . . . . . . . . . . . . . . . . . . . . . . . . . . .43
Initial Consonant: /l/*l* . . . . . . . . . . . . . . . . . . . . . . . . . . . . . . . . . . . . . . . . . . . . . . . . . . . . . . . . . . . .44
Auditory Discrimination: /o/*o* . . . . . . . . . . . . . . . . . . . . . . . . . . . . . . . . . . . . . . . . . . . . . . . . . . . . . . .45
Initial Vowel: /o/*o* . . . . . . . . . . . . . . . . . . . . . . . . . . . . . . . . . . . . . . . . . . . . . . . . . . . . . . . . . . . . . . .46
Initial Consonants Review: /j/*j*, /m/*m*, /p/*p*, /l/*l* . . . . . . . . . . . . . . . . . . . . . . . . . . . . . . . . . . . . . .47
Listening, Speaking, Viewing . . . . . . . . . . . . . . . . . . . . . . . . . . . . . . . . . . . . . . . . . . . . . . . . . . . . . . . .48
Letter Identification: *K, R, S, V, I* . . . . . . . . . . . . . . . . . . . . . . . . . . . . . . . . . . . . . . . . . . . . . . . . . . . .49
Letter Identification: *k, r, s, v, i* . . . . . . . . . . . . . . . . . . . . . . . . . . . . . . . . . . . . . . . . . . . . . . . . . . . . .50
Auditory Discrimination: /k/*k* . . . . . . . . . . . . . . . . . . . . . . . . . . . . . . . . . . . . . . . . . . . . . . . . . . . . . . .51
Initial Consonant: /k/*k* . . . . . . . . . . . . . . . . . . . . . . . . . . . . . . . . . . . . . . . . . . . . . . . . . . . . . . . . . . .52
Auditory Discrimination: /r/*r* . . . . . . . . . . . . . . . . . . . . . . . . . . . . . . . . . . . . . . . . . . . . . . . . . . . . . . . .53
Initial Consonant: /r/*r* . . . . . . . . . . . . . . . . . . . . . . . . . . . . . . . . . . . . . . . . . . . . . . . . . . . . . . . . . . . .54
Auditory Discrimination: /s/*s* . . . . . . . . . . . . . . . . . . . . . . . . . . . . . . . . . . . . . . . . . . . . . . . . . . . . . . .55
Initial Consonant: /s/*s* . . . . . . . . . . . . . . . . . . . . . . . . . . . . . . . . . . . . . . . . . . . . . . . . . . . . . . . . . . .56
Auditory Discrimination: /v/*v* . . . . . . . . . . . . . . . . . . . . . . . . . . . . . . . . . . . . . . . . . . . . . . . . . . . . . . .57
Initial Consonant: /v/*v* . . . . . . . . . . . . . . . . . . . . . . . . . . . . . . . . . . . . . . . . . . . . . . . . . . . . . . . . . . .58
Auditory Discrimination: /i/*i* . . . . . . . . . . . . . . . . . . . . . . . . . . . . . . . . . . . . . . . . . . . . . . . . . . . . . . . .59
Initial Vowel: /i/*i* . . . . . . . . . . . . . . . . . . . . . . . . . . . . . . . . . . . . . . . . . . . . . . . . . . . . . . . . . . . . . . . .60
Initial Consonants Review: /k/*k*, /r/*r*, /s/*s*, /v/*v* . . . . . . . . . . . . . . . . . . . . . . . . . . . . . . . . . . . . . .61
Listening, Speaking, Viewing . . . . . . . . . . . . . . . . . . . . . . . . . . . . . . . . . . . . . . . . . . . . . . . . . . . . . . . .62
Letter Identification: *Q, W, Y, Z, U* . . . . . . . . . . . . . . . . . . . . . . . . . . . . . . . . . . . . . . . . . . . . . . . . . . .63
Letter Identification: *q, w, y, z, u* . . . . . . . . . . . . . . . . . . . . . . . . . . . . . . . . . . . . . . . . . . . . . . . . . . . .64
Auditory Discrimination: /kw/*qu* . . . . . . . . . . . . . . . . . . . . . . . . . . . . . . . . . . . . . . . . . . . . . . . . . . . . . .65
Initial Consonant: /kw/*qu* . . . . . . . . . . . . . . . . . . . . . . . . . . . . . . . . . . . . . . . . . . . . . . . . . . . . . . . . . .66
Auditory Discrimination: /w/*w* . . . . . . . . . . . . . . . . . . . . . . . . . . . . . . . . . . . . . . . . . . . . . . . . . . . . . . .67
Initial Consonant: /w/*w* . . . . . . . . . . . . . . . . . . . . . . . . . . . . . . . . . . . . . . . . . . . . . . . . . . . . . . . . . . .68
Auditory Discrimination: /y/*y* . . . . . . . . . . . . . . . . . . . . . . . . . . . . . . . . . . . . . . . . . . . . . . . . . . . . . . . .69
Initial Consonant: /y/*y* . . . . . . . . . . . . . . . . . . . . . . . . . . . . . . . . . . . . . . . . . . . . . . . . . . . . . . . . . . . .70
Auditory Discrimination: /z/*z* . . . . . . . . . . . . . . . . . . . . . . . . . . . . . . . . . . . . . . . . . . . . . . . . . . . . . . . .71
Initial Consonant: /z/*z* . . . . . . . . . . . . . . . . . . . . . . . . . . . . . . . . . . . . . . . . . . . . . . . . . . . . . . . . . . . .72
Auditory Discrimination: /u/*u* . . . . . . . . . . . . . . . . . . . . . . . . . . . . . . . . . . . . . . . . . . . . . . . . . . . . . . .73
Initial Vowel: /u/*u* . . . . . . . . . . . . . . . . . . . . . . . . . . . . . . . . . . . . . . . . . . . . . . . . . . . . . . . . . . . . . . .74
Initial Consonants Review: /kw/*qu*, /w/*w*, /y/*y*, /z/*z* . . . . . . . . . . . . . . . . . . . . . . . . . . . . . . . . . . .75
My Notes . . . . . . . . . . . . . . . . . . . . . . . . . . . . . . . . . . . . . . . . . . . . . . . . . . . . . . . . . . . . . . . . . . . .76-80

# Listening, Speaking, Viewing

Listening, Speaking, Viewing
5

## OBJECTIVES

Listening, Speaking, Viewing Skills

Apply Comprehension Strategies
in Viewing Activities

Predict outcomes

## MATERIALS

*Zoo-Be-Doo* Big Book, crayons

## ACTIVITIES — BUILD BACKGROUND

- Read the poem "Counting at the Zoo" to the children. Then read the poem again, inviting children to recite and follow these finger motions.

**Counting at the Zoo**

One, one; the zoo is lots of fun!
    (Hold up one finger.)
Two, two; see a kangaroo!
    (Hold up two fingers.)
Three, three; see a chimpanzee!
    (Hold up three fingers.)
Four, four; hear the lion's roar!
    (Hold up four fingers.)
Five, five; watch the seals dive!
    (Hold up five fingers.)
Six, six; there's a monkey doing tricks!
    (Hold up six fingers.)
Seven, seven; elephant's eleven!
    (Hold up seven fingers.)
Eight, eight; a tiger and his mate!
    (Hold up eight fingers.)
Nine, nine; penguins in a line!
    (Hold up nine fingers.)
Ten, ten; I want to come again!
    (Hold up ten fingers.)

- Invite children to name types of animals that they might see at the zoo.

## ACTIVITIES — READ THE BIG BOOK

- Display the Big Book *Zoo-Be-Doo* and read the title, pointing to each word as you read aloud. Then point out the name of the author and illustrator. Invite children to predict what the story will be about.
- Write the number 5 on the chalkboard. Have children find page 5 in their books. Have them look at the bottom of each page to find the page numbers. Discuss the picture with the children

by asking questions such as: *Who is the lady in the gold uniform? Why is she dressed in a uniform? Where does she work? What do you think she is looking for? Where do you think the keys are?*

- Read *Zoo-Be-Doo* to the children. As you read, point to each line of text, emphasizing that stories are read from left to right and from top to bottom.
- Encourage children to chime in as they become familiar with the predictable pattern of the story.
- From time to time, pause and let children predict where the keys might be found. At the end of the story, ask if they were surprised by the ending, and have them explain their answers.

## ACTIVITIES — RESPOND TO THE BIG BOOK

- Children may enjoy drawing pictures of favorite zoo animals in their Journals. Some children may also wish to copy words from the zoo web.
- Invite children to retell their favorite part of the story and to explain why they enjoyed that part.

## ACTIVITIES — REPEATED READINGS

- Reread *Zoo-Be-Doo* with the children. Use your hand to track each line. Stop two or three times during the story to invite children to read a page on their own.
- Reread *Zoo-Be-Doo* with the children. Engage them in brief discussions as the story progresses. Help them recognize the different ways in which the animals showed that they "did not know." You may wish to have several children act out the story as you read it.

# Listening, Speaking, Viewing

6

Listening, Speaking, Viewing

Macmillan/McGraw-Hill

## OBJECTIVES

Listening, Speaking, Viewing Skills

Apply Comprehension Strategies
in Viewing Activities

Draw conclusions

Identify picture details

Compare and contrast

## MATERIALS

*Zoo-Be-Doo* Little Books, picture of a
bird's nest, chart paper, paint,
paintbrushes, colored chalk, crayons,
mural paper, letter cards for *a, n, t, b, c*

- Display a picture of a bird's nest. Encourage a discussion about nests: what they are made of, where they are found, which animals build nests, why animals build nests.
- Distribute copies of the Little Book, *Zoo-Be-Doo*, and have children flip through the pages looking for a nest. They should discover that a quail has built a nest for her chick on page 28. Ask children to tell what they see in the picture. Help children learn more about quails.

## DEVELOP/APPLY

### Use the Page
- Write the number 6 on the chalkboard and say it aloud. Have children turn to page 6 in their books.
- Look at the picture together with the children. Explain that the children are in the Activity Room at the zoo: a place where they may take part in zoo activities such as painting, drawing, watching films, making models, and listening to animal handlers talk about the animals. Invite children to describe the activities they see in the picture.
- Have children identify the animals shown in the picture. After the animals have been identified, pose riddles about each animal and have children guess the animal's name.
  For example: *This animal has a hump on its back. This animal is in the cat family. This animal lays eggs.*
- Ask children to look at the tiger and the camel. Help children compare the animals by asking questions such as: *How are these animals alike?* (4 legs) *Where does a tiger live? Where does a camel live?* Discuss the similarities and differences among the other animals.

### Writing
As a shared writing experience, invite children to help you write a list of animals that build nests. Call on volunteers to illustrate the list.

- Assign small groups. Distribute mural paper, paint, paintbrushes, colored chalk, and crayons to each group. Have children use the materials to create a mural of zoo animals. You might want to display the picture on page 6 as a model.
- Children may enjoy reading books about the animals in this picture. You may begin with the following books:

**Fiction**
*How the Camel Got Its Hump* by Rudyard Kipling (Rabbit Ears, 1989).

*The Three Bears* by Paul Galdone (Clarion, 1972).

**Nonfiction**
*Alligators* by Christine Butterworth (Steck Vaughn, 1990).

*Tigers* by Kate Petty (Barrons, 1991).

*Big Cats* by Joyce Milton (G. P. Putnam's Sons, 1994).

*Never Kiss an Alligator!* by Colleen Stanley Bare (Puffin, 1989).

*How to Hide a Polar Bear* by Ruth Heller (G. P. Putnam's Sons, 1995).

- Have children recall the animals and objects shown on page 6. Write the words on chart paper as you read them aloud: *tiger, camel, bear, alligator, nest, egg, easel, paint, posters, boys, girls.* Display the letter cards *a, n, t, b, c.* Have children find the letters in these words on the chart and then draw a line under each.

# Letter Identification: *B, C, T, N, A*

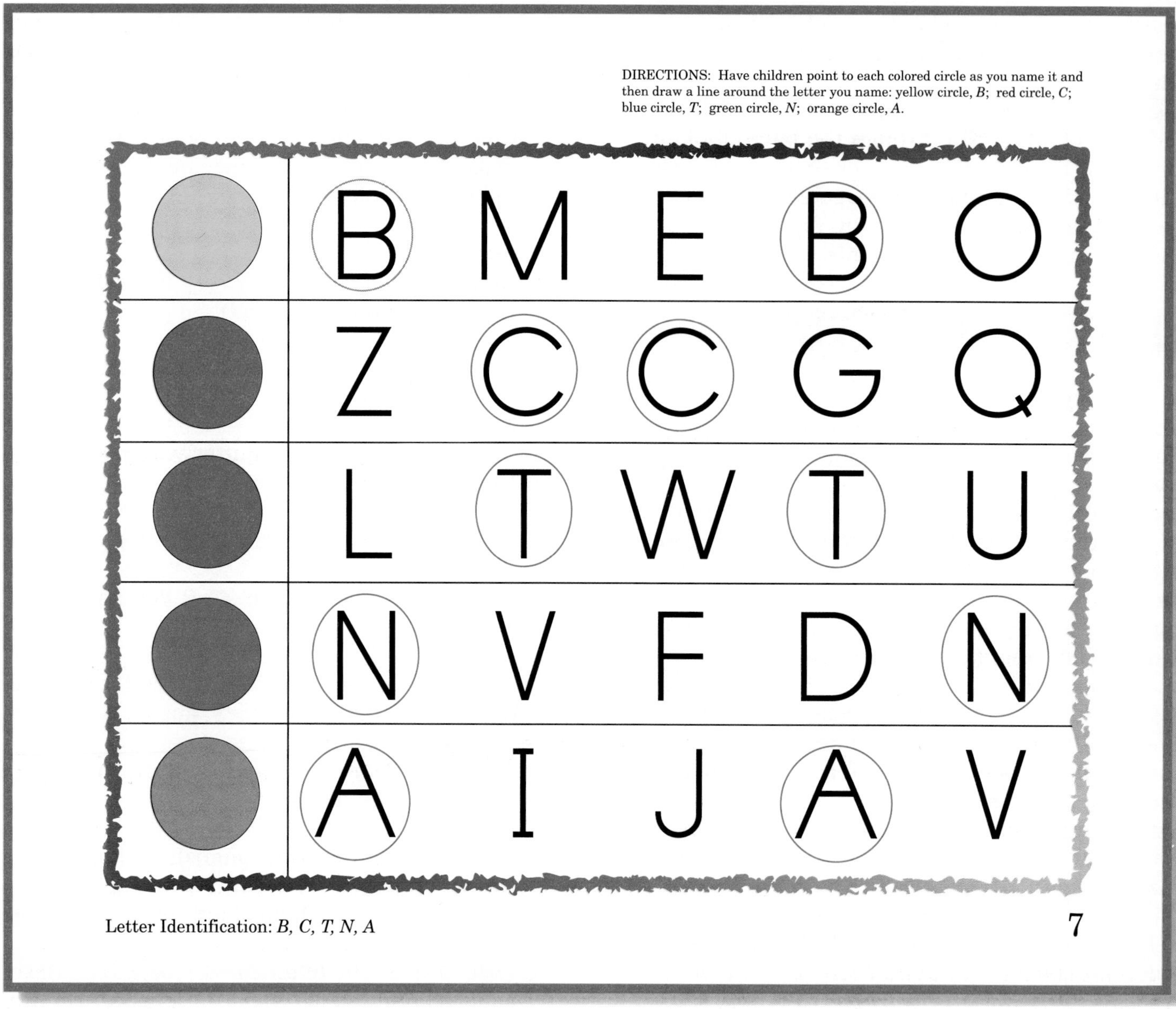

DIRECTIONS: Have children point to each colored circle as you name it and then draw a line around the letter you name: yellow circle, *B*; red circle, *C*; blue circle, *T*; green circle, *N*; orange circle, *A*.

| | | | | | |
|---|---|---|---|---|---|
| ⬤ | B | M | E | Ⓑ | O |
| ⬤ | Z | Ⓒ | Ⓒ | G | Q |
| ⬤ | L | Ⓣ | W | Ⓣ | U |
| ⬤ | Ⓝ | V | F | D | Ⓝ |
| ⬤ | Ⓐ | I | J | Ⓐ | V |

Letter Identification: *B, C, T, N, A*

7

## OBJECTIVES

Phonics and Decoding Skills

Identify capital letters: *B, C, T, N, A*

## MATERIALS

ABC cards or letter cards for *B, C, T, N, A;* assorted picture books; scissors; magazines; newspapers; paste; large sheets of drawing paper

- Write a simple sentence on the chalkboard such as *Today is Tuesday.* or *We are in school.* and read it aloud to children. Explain that written words are made up of letters and that by knowing letters and words, they can learn to read. Tell children that today they will be learning the names of some letters.
- Display a letter card for *B* and ask children to name the letter (capital *B*). Follow a similar procedure for the letters *C, T, N,* and *A.* Then write the names of children in the class that begin with any of the above letters. Underline the capital letter in each name as you write it on the chalkboard.
- Distribute letter cards *B, C, T, N,* and *A,* one to each child. Write one of the letters on the chalkboard. Ask children who are holding the same letter card to stand up and show their letters. Then have children say the name of the letter aloud. Continue the activity by writing each of the letters on the chalkboard.

## DEVELOP/APPLY

### Use the Page
- Write the number 7 on the chalkboard and say it aloud. Have children turn to page 7 in their books.
- Have children find and point to the yellow circle in the first row. Invite children to name the letters they know.
- Ask children to name the letter in the first row that has a line around it (capital *B*). Then have children draw a line around each capital *B* in the row.
- Next, ask children to point to the red circle in the second row and name the letters they know. Then have them draw a line around each capital *C.*
- In the row with the blue circle, have children draw a line around each capital *T.*
- Continue in this manner with the two remaining rows for letters *N* and *A.*

- Randomly display capital letter cards for *B, C, T, N,* and *A* along the chalkboard ledge. As you call out the name of a letter, have a child come up to the chalkboard, hold up the correct letter card, and say the letter name.

  To vary the activity, give directions such as the following:
  **1.** Name the letter between capital *B* and capital *T.*
  **2.** Name the letter to the right (left) of capital *N.*
  **3.** Name the first (last) letter.
  Periodically rearrange the order of the letters.

- Display a variety of picture books around the room that contain words in the titles with capital letters *B, C, T, N,* and *A.* Give pairs of children a capital letter card for one of the letters and invite them to go capital letter hunting. When they find the capital letter, have them point to the letter in the title and say it aloud.
- Help children form small groups. Provide each group with scissors, magazines, newspapers, paste, and a large sheet of drawing paper with one of the following capital letters written on it: *B, C, T, N, A.* Then invite children to find examples of their assigned letters, cut them out, and paste them on their papers to make a capital letter collage.

#### Second-Language Support
Children who are accustomed to a different alphabet may have difficulty identifying letters. Create one set of letter cards for each child. Display *B, C, T, N,* and *A* in a row. Then ask children to match their set of letters with your row.

# Letter Identification: *b, c, t, n, a*

DIRECTIONS: Have children point to each colored circle as you name it and then draw a line around the letter you name: yellow circle, *b*; red circle, *c*; blue circle, *t*; green circle, *n*; orange circle, *a*.

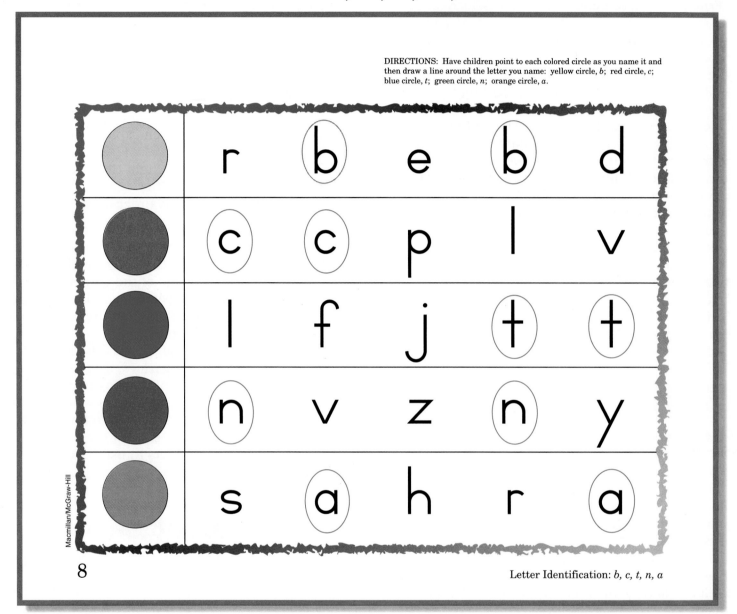

8

Letter Identification: *b, c, t, n, a*

Macmillan/McGraw-Hill

## OBJECTIVES

Phonics and Decoding Skills

Identify lowercase letters: *b, c, t, n, a*

## MATERIALS

ABC cards or letter cards for *b, c, t, n, a;* chart paper; marker; crayons

## BUILD BACKGROUND

- Encourage children to point out letters and words they see around the room. Emphasize how letters work together to form the words we read.
- Display a letter card for lowercase *b* and have it identified. Have children repeat the letter name. Then, invite children to look around the classroom to find examples of lowercase *b* printed on charts, labels, and so on. Repeat the procedure with the lowercase letters *c, t, n,* and *a.*
- Distribute letter cards for lowercase letters *b, c, t, n,* and *a,* so that each child has a card. Name one of the letters and ask children who have that letter to hold it up and say the name of the letter aloud. Continue with the remaining letters.

## DEVELOP/APPLY

### Use the Page

- Write the number 8 on the chalkboard and say it aloud. Have children turn to page 8 in their books.
- Have children find and point to the yellow circle in the first row. Invite children to name the letters they know.
- Ask children to name the letter in the first row that has a line around it (lowercase *b*). Then have children draw a line around each lowercase *b* in the row.
- Next, ask children to point to the red circle in the second row and name the letters they know. Then have them draw a line around each lowercase *c.*
- In the row with the blue circle, have children name the letters they know and then draw a line around each lowercase *t.*
- Continue in a similar manner with the two remaining rows for letters *n* and *a.*

## REINFORCE

- Distribute letter cards *b, c, t, n,* and *a* to the children. Have five volunteers stand in various locations around the room, each holding a different letter card. As you say a letter, have all the children who have that letter join the child with the same letter and together say the letter aloud. Continue with the remaining letters.
- Use black marker to randomly print the lowercase letters *b, c, t, n,* and *a* on three sheets of chart paper. Then name a letter and have three volunteers go to each chart and trace over the letter with a crayon of a different color. Continue until all the letters are identified.
- Use lowercase letter cards *b, c, t, n,* and *a* and capital letter cards *B, C, T, N,* and *A.* Then invite children to play the following game. Explain that you will hold up a letter card. If the letter card has a lowercase letter, they are to say its name in a soft voice. If the letter card shows a capital letter, they are to say its name in a loud voice.

# Auditory Discimination: /b/*b*

DIRECTIONS: Help children identify the key picture at the top of the page. Then have them draw a line around the pictures that begin with the same sound as the word *box*. Have children think of other words that begin with the same sound as *box*.

Auditory Discrimination: /b/*b*     Children should also circle bat, ball, boy, bear, bees, beehive.     9

## OBJECTIVES

Phonics and Decoding Skills

Discriminate among initial sounds

Discriminate among final sounds

## MATERIALS

Picture or illustration of a box, a large cardboard box, marker, magazines, scissors, ball, glue

## BUILD BACKGROUND

- Display a picture or an illustration of a box, and ask children to identify it. Tell children to listen as you say the words *box* and *ball.* Ask if the two words begin with the same sound. Have children repeat the words. Then, say the word *cat,* and ask if the word begins with the same sound as *box.* Encourage children to think of other words that begin like *box.*
- Say the following pairs of words. Have children clap their hands once when both words begin with the same sound as box. Use these word pairs: *box, balloon; box, table; box, baby; box, nail; box, button; box, cat; box, apple; box, bug.*

## DEVELOP/APPLY

### Use the Page

- Write the number 9 on the chalkboard. Ask children to turn to page 9 in their books.
- Point to the key picture at the top of the page and have children identify it as a box. Then, invite children to describe the scene by telling a story about the boy and the bear. If they do not mention it, point out that the boy and bear are playing ball. Encourage children to include the different things they see in the picture, such as the bat, cat, ball, butterfly, and worm.
- Have children point to the butterfly. Ask why a line is drawn around the picture. (*Butterfly* begins with the same sound as *box.*) Have children say the two words again and then trace over the line with a pencil.
- Have children complete the page by drawing a line around each object whose name begins with the same sound as *box.*

## REINFORCE

- Place a large cardboard box on a table in front of the room with the letter *b* written on it. Provide children with magazines and scissors. Invite children to cut out magazine pictures of objects whose names begin with the same sound as *box.* Then have children take turns holding up their pictures for the class to identify before gluing them on the box.

  To vary the activity, have volunteers choose a picture from the box, say its name, and identify the beginning sound.
- Invite children to play "Name the /b/ Word." Explain that you will say a group of words and they must say the word in each group that begins with /b/b. Possible word groups are:

  | | | |
  |---|---|---|
  | doll | cat | ball |
  | needle | button | yarn |
  | baby | cup | towel |

- Help children form two lines, each facing the other, for a game of "Bounce the Ball." Give a ball to the first child in either line. Tell the child to say a word that begins like *box* and then toss the ball so it bounces once to the first child in the opposite line. That player, in turn, says a word that begins like *box* before tossing the ball to the next child in line on the opposite side. Continue until each child has a chance to name a word and bounce the ball.

## CHALLENGE

### Final Consonant: /b/b

Invite children to listen to the following words: *web, tab, rib, cob, tub.* Encourage children to tell how the words are alike. (They all end with /b/b.)

Follow the same procedure with these words: *bed, bat, big, box, bus.* Children should recognize that they begin with /b/. Point out that /b/ can begin and end words. Then randomly say each word again and have children tell if the word begins or ends with /b/.

# Initial Consonant: /b/*b*

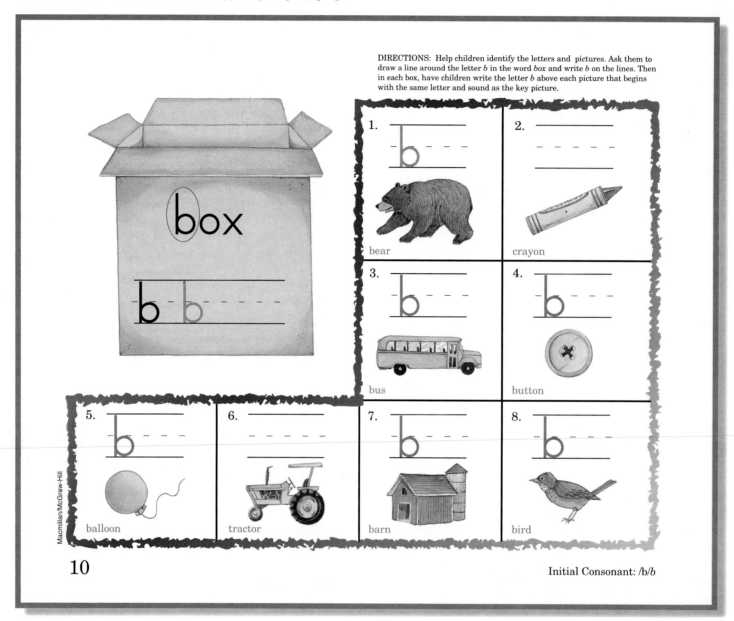

DIRECTIONS: Help children identify the letters and pictures. Ask them to draw a line around the letter *b* in the word *box* and write *b* on the lines. Then in each box, have children write the letter *b* above each picture that begins with the same letter and sound as the key picture.

box

b b

1.
b
bear

2.
crayon

3.
b
bus

4.
b
button

5.
b
balloon

6.
tractor

7.
b
barn

8.
b
bird

Macmillan/McGraw-Hill

10

Initial Consonant: /b/*b*

## OBJECTIVES

Phonics and Decoding Skills

Recognize initial consonant: /b/*b*

Recognize final consonant: /b/*b*

## MATERIALS

ABC cards or letter cards for *B* and *b*, clay or salt dough, marker, blank cards, construction paper, magazines, newspapers, store flyers, scissors, stapler or tape, classroom objects that begin with /b/*b*

- Display letter cards *B* and *b*. As you point to each letter in turn, encourage volunteers to identify them as capital *B* or lowercase *b*. Say the word *box*. Elicit from children that the word begins with the letter *b*. Write the word *box* on the chalkboard and point to the letter *b*.
- Ask children to clap their hands when they hear you say words that begin with /b/*b*.

## DEVELOP/APPLY

### Use the Page
- Write the number 10 on the chalkboard and say it aloud. Have children turn to page 10 in their books.
- Direct attention to the key picture and ask children to identify the letter that begins the word *box* and then draw a line around the letter *b*.
- Point to the letter *b* on the lines in the box. Have children identify the *b*. Invite them to trace the letter, starting at the red dot. You may wish to demonstrate the proper way to form the letter on the chalkboard. Then have children write the letter *b*.
- Ask children to point to the picture of the bear. Have them say *box* and *bear*. Ask if the two words begin with the same letter and sound. Then point out the letter *b* above the bear and have children trace over it with a pencil.
- Point out the remaining boxes and challenge children to identify the picture in each one. Explain that they will write *b* above each picture that begins with the same letter and sound as *box*.

### Reading
Invite children to look through the Big Book or Little Book *Zoo-Be-Doo* and find words that begin with /b/*b*.

### Writing
Have pairs of children create pictures of words whose names begin with *b*. Help them label their pictures.

- Invite children to make the letter *b* out of clay or salt dough. Ask them to create a sculpture of an object whose name begins with /b/*b*. If children need help getting started, you may wish to suggest the following: *bear, bug, banana, boat*. Display children's work and help them make labels.
- Make and display a large construction paper basket on the bulletin board, or use a small wicker or straw basket. Point out that *basket* begins with /b/*b*. Distribute magazines, newspapers, store flyers, and scissors to children. Invite them to fill the basket with pictures of items that begin with *b*. Have children share the pictures they find, and name their pictures before they put them in the basket.
- Invite children to play "Do You See What I See?" Explain that you will tell about something you see in the classroom that begins with /b/*b* as in *box*, and they will have to guess what it is. As children name each object, write the word on the chalkboard and have a volunteer underline the letter *b*.
 **1.** I see a place where we hang our pictures. Do you see what I see? (bulletin board)
 **2.** I see something to read. Do you see what I see? (book)
 **3.** I see something that bounces. Do you see what I see? ( ball)

Invite children to make up their own clues.

### Final Consonant: /b/*b*
Ask children to listen for the /b/*b* sound as you say the following word pairs: *bat, tub; big, cub; bed, cab; box, rib; bug, web*. Challenge them to discover that one word begins with /b/*b* and the other ends with /b/*b*. Write the word pairs on the chalkboard. Point to each word and say them aloud with the children. Invite volunteers to underline the letter *b* in each word.

# Auditory Discrimination: /k/c

DIRECTIONS: Help children identify the key picture at the top of the page. Then have them draw a line around the pictures that begin with the same sound as the word *cup*. Have children think of other words that begin with the same sound as *cup*.

Auditory Discrimination: /k/c        Children should also circle cow, cake, candles, camera, cap, cat.        11

## OBJECTIVES

Phonics and Decoding Skills

Discriminate among initial sounds

## MATERIALS

Picture or illustration of a cup, pictures or illustrations of objects that begin with /k/c and other initial consonant sounds, beanbag

- Display a picture of a cup, and ask children to identify it. Tell them to listen as you say the words *cup* and *car.* Ask if the words begin with the same sound. Have children repeat the words. Then say the word *box,* and ask whether it begins with the same sound as the word *cup.*
- Say the following pairs of words and invite children to stand when they hear a pair that begins with the same sound. Use these word pairs: *cup, cow; cup, baby; cup, cap; cup, nail; cup, cookie; cup, apple; cup, table; cup, capital.* Have children think of other words that begin with /k/*c.*

## DEVELOP/APPLY

### Use the Page
- Write the number 11 on the chalkboard, and have children turn to page 11 in their books.
- Point to the key picture at the top of the page and have children identify it as a cup. Then, invite children to describe the scene by telling a story about Cow's birthday party. You may wish to prompt children with these questions: *Who are Cow's friends? How many candles are on Cow's cake? What is Dog doing? What is Dog wearing on his head? What is Cat eating?* Encourage children to identify the different things they see in the picture, such as the cow, cake, candles, camera, cat, cone, cap, dog, bird, and presents.
- Have children point to the ice cream cone. Encourage them to tell why a line has been drawn around it. (*Cone* begins with the same sound as *cup.*) Have children say the words *cup* and *cone,* and then write over the line using their pencils.
- Then have children complete the page by drawing a line around each picture whose name begins with the same sound as *cup.* Have children think of other words that begin with /k/*c.*

- Randomly display pictures or illustrations of things that begin with /k/*c* and other initial consonant sounds, such as a cat, coat, coins, cup, bear, book, table, tent, nail, napkin. Ask children to identify the pictures. Then hold up the picture of the cat and have children name all the other pictures that begin with /k/*c.*

To extend the activity, make up a sentence for each /k/*c* word. Have children repeat the words they hear that begin with /k/*c.* Possible sentences are:
1. Carla's cat caught a mouse.
2. My new coat has blue cuffs and a collar.
3. My cousin collects old coins.
4. We had a cup of cocoa.

- Explain that as you walk around the classroom, you will point to and name different objects. Tell children to clap their hands three times when they hear you say a word that begins like *cup.* Possible objects may include the following: calendar, crayon, can, cup, cage, container, car, card, case, coat, comb, cookie, candy.
- Have children form a circle. Choose a volunteer to stand in the middle of the circle. Explain that he or she will toss a beanbag to a child and say, "C is for __." The child who catches the beanbag must then say a word that begins like *cup.* If the child responds correctly, he or she stands in the middle of the circle and the game continues.
- To reinforce the /k/ sound, have children learn to sing the Australian round, "Kookaburra," from **Sing a Sound Audiocassette,** Tape 2, Side 1.

# Initial Consonant: /k/c

DIRECTIONS: Help children identify the letters and pictures. Ask them to draw a line around the letter *c* in the word *cup* and write *c* on the lines. Then in each box, have children write the letter *c* above each picture that begins with the same letter and sound as the key picture.

cup
c   C

1. ____ C
car

2. ____
football

3. ____ C
carrot

4. ____ C
camera

5. ____
watermelon

6. ____ C
cactus

7. ____ C
camel

8. ____ C
cave

Macmillan/McGraw-Hill

12

Initial Consonant: /k/c

## OBJECTIVES

Phonics and Decoding Skills

Recognize initial consonant: /k/c

## MATERIALS

ABC cards or letter cards for *C* and *c*, cardboard stencil for *c*, drawing paper, crayons, scissors, magazines, paste, pictures from books and magazines showing objects that begin with *c*

- Display letter cards for *C* and *c*. Point to each letter and have children identify them as capital *C* and lowercase *c*. Say the word *cup*. Elicit from children that *cup* begins with the letter *c*. Write the word *cup* on the chalkboard and have a volunteer circle the letter *c*.
- Tell children to stand up when they hear a word that begins with the same letter and sound as *cup*. Use these words: *car, dish, cow, camera, card, radio, coat, can.*

## DEVELOP/APPLY

### Use the Page
- Write the number 12 on the chalkboard and say it aloud. Have children turn to page 12 in their books.
- Direct attention to the key picture and ask children to identify the letter that begins the word *cup* and then draw a line around the letter *c*.
- Point to the letter *c* on the lines in the cup, and have children identify the *c*. Have children write over the letter, starting at the red dot, as you demonstrate the proper letter formation on the chalkboard. Then have children write the letter *c*.
- Ask children to point to the picture of the car. Have them say *cup* and *car.* Ask if the two words begin with the same letter and sound. Then point out the letter *c* above the car and have children write over it with a pencil.
- Point out the remaining boxes and invite children to identify the picture in each one. Explain that they will write *c* above each picture that begins with the same letter and sound as *cup.*

### Reading
Invite children to look for words in the classroom that begin with /k/*c*. Help them read the words.

### Writing
Have children copy any words they find in the classroom that begin with /k/*c* onto a Journal Page.

**REINFORCE**

- Make and distribute cardboard stencils for *c*, drawing paper, crayons, and scissors. Have children use the stencils to make, decorate, and cut out *c*'s for the border of a bulletin board display. Then, provide children with magazines, scissors, paste, and more drawing paper. Have them cut out pictures of objects that begin with the same letter and sound as *cup* and paste each one on a separate sheet of paper. Encourage children to then write the letter *c* under each picture. Invite them to hang their pictures on the bulletin board.
- Invite children to draw and color a picture of something that begins with /k/*c*, such as a car, cat, cup, cap, cape, corn, cow, coat, cake. Help children label their pictures. Then randomly display their pictures along the chalkboard ledge. Name a picture and have a volunteer find it, hold it up, and say the letter and sound that begins its name.
- Write words that begin with *c* on the chalkboard. Point to each word and have it read. Then make up a riddle about one of the words on the chalkboard, such as: *I have four wheels. I can stop and go. What am I?* (car) Have the class call out the correct answer. Point to the word on the board, and have a volunteer underline the initial *c*.

**MEETING INDIVIDUAL NEEDS**

**Second-Language Support**
Non-native speakers may need additional support in identifying objects that begin with /k/*c*. Pair native and non-native English speakers to match letters and objects.

# Auditory Discrimination: /t/t

DIRECTIONS: Help children identify the key picture at the top of the page. Then have them draw a line around the pictures that begin with the same sound as the word *tent*. Have children think of other words that begin with the same sound as *tent*.

Auditory Discrimination: /t/t          Children should also circle tiger, turtle, taco, table, toaster, toast, towel, tulips.          13

## OBJECTIVES

Phonics and Decoding Skills

Discriminate among initial sounds

Discriminate among final sounds

## MATERIALS

Picture or illustration of a tent, pictures or objects that begin with *t* and objects that begin with other consonant sounds, tape recorder

- Display a picture of a tent and have it identified. Ask children to tell how people use tents. Then have children listen as you say *tent* and *tiger.* Ask if the two words begin with the same sound. Have children repeat the words. Then say the word *cup* and ask if this word begins with the same sound as *tent.* Call on volunteers to think of other words that begin like *tent.*
- Say the following pairs of words and invite children to tap a pencil on the desk two times when they hear a word pair that begins with the same sound as *tent.* Use these word pairs: *tent, toe; turtle, ant; top, tight; tooth, ball; table, tomato; telephone, nickel; tool, camp.*

## DEVELOP/APPLY

### Use the Page
- Write the number 13 on the chalkboard. Ask children to turn to page 13 in their books.
- Point to the key picture at the top of the page and have it identified. Then, invite children to tell a story about the picture. You may wish to include prompts such as the following: *What animal characters do you see? Where are they sitting? What is Tiger doing? What is Turtle doing? What do you think they are making? What ingredients are they using?* Help children identify the different things they see in the picture.
- Ask children to find the picture of the tomato and tell why there is a line drawn around it (*Tomato* begins with the same sound as *tent.*) Have children say the words *tent* and *tomato* and then trace over the line using their pencils.
- Then have children complete the page by drawing a line around each object whose name begins with the same sound as *tent.*

- Invite small groups of children to make up a *t* story. One child begins with a sentence that includes a word with initial /t/*t.* You may wish to suggest story starters such as the following: *Once upon a time, a tiny turtle named . . . Long ago, in the town of . . .* Have each child, in turn, add to the story with a sentence that includes at least one word with initial /t/*t.*
- If possible, tape record the children's *t* stories. As you play back the tape, have children listen to each story and identify the *t* words they hear by holding up a *t* letter card.
- Gather a variety of objects or pictures of objects that begin with /t/*t,* such as a top, tie, towel, toothbrush, teabag, and objects or pictures of objects that begin with other consonant sounds. Place all objects/pictures in a large paper bag. Call on volunteers, in turn, to take out an object. Have the class name the object and tell whether or not it begins with /t/*t.*

### Final Consonant: /t/*t*
Invite children to listen to these words and then repeat each one after you: *bat, net, sit, pot, cut.* Ask how the words are alike.

Then have volunteers form a line. Say a word and ask each child if the word begins or ends with /t/. After the child responds, he or she sits down. Continue with other volunteers. Possible words: *sit, ten, top, mat, cat, tug, not, fat, toad, vet.*

# Initial Consonant: /t/*t*

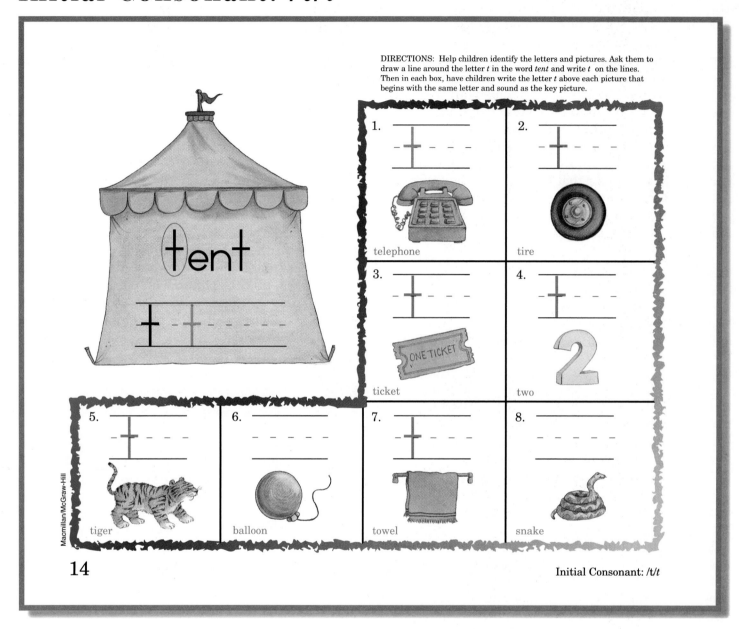

DIRECTIONS: Help children identify the letters and pictures. Ask them to draw a line around the letter *t* in the word *tent* and write *t* on the lines. Then in each box, have children write the letter *t* above each picture that begins with the same letter and sound as the key picture.

tent

1. telephone
2. tire
3. ticket
4. two
5. tiger
6. balloon
7. towel
8. snake

Macmillan/McGraw-Hill

14

Initial Consonant: /t/*t*

## OBJECTIVES

Phonics and Decoding Skills

Recognize initial consonant: /t/*t*

Recognize final consonant: /t/*t*

## MATERIALS

ABC cards or letter cards for *T* and *t*, magazines, newspapers, store flyers, scissors, paste, cardboard or oaktag, drawing paper, crayons

## BUILD BACKGROUND

- Display letter cards for *T* and *t*. Point to each letter and have children identify them as capital *T* and lowercase *t*. Tell children that the word *tent* begins with the letter *t*. Write the word *tent* on the chalkboard and point to the letter *t*.
- Provide each child with a letter card for *t*. Ask children to hold up the letter card when they hear you say a word that begins like *tent*.

## DEVELOP/APPLY

### Use the Page
- Write the number 14 on the chalkboard and say it aloud. Ask children to turn to page 14 in their books.
- Direct children's attention to the key picture and ask children to identify the letter that begins the word *tent*, and then draw a line around the letter *t*.
- Point to the letter *t* on the lines in the tent. Have children identify the *t*. Invite them to trace the letter, starting at the red dot. You may wish to demonstrate the proper way to form the letter on the chalkboard. Then have children write the letter *t*.
- Ask children to point to the picture of the telephone. Have them say *tent* and *telephone* and then decide whether the two words begin with the same letter and sound. Point out the letter *t* above the telephone and have children trace over it with a pencil.
- Invite children to identify the pictures in the remaining boxes and then write *t* above each picture that begins with the same letter and sound as *tent*.

### Reading
Invite children to look for words around the classroom that begin with /t/*t*.

### Writing
Have children use their Journals and write a word that begins with /t/*t* and then use it in a sentence.

## REINFORCE

- Provide children with magazines, newspapers, store flyers, scissors, paste, and drawing paper. Have children write *t* at the top of their papers. Children then draw or cut out and paste pictures of objects that begin with /t/*t*.
- Provide cardboard patterns of T-shirts and ties. Have children trace one of the shapes onto drawing paper and then cut it out. They may decorate their ties or shirts by writing *t*, using crayons of different colors.
- Help children think of words that begin with /t/*t* as in *tent*. Write their responses on the chalkboard. Then point to each word and have children repeat the word after you. Call on volunteers to circle the *t* in each word. Then ask children to choose two words from the board and copy them onto their papers.

## CHALLENGE

**Final Consonant:** /t/*t*
Say these words aloud and ask children if each ends with the same sound and letter as *sit: got, cat, nut, bat*. Write *sit, goat, cat, pat* on the chalkboard and have children identify the final letter and sound. Then have children think of words that rhyme with *cat, met, not, sit,* and *nut*.

# Auditory Discrimination: /n/*n*

DIRECTIONS: Help children identify the key picture at the top of the page. Then have them draw a line around the pictures that begin with the same sound as the word *notebook*. Have children think of other words that begin with the same sound as *notebook*.

Auditory Discrimination: /n/*n*     Children should also circle nest, nuts, napkin, nurse, newspaper, noodles, knife.     15

## OBJECTIVES

Phonics and Decoding Skills

Discriminate among initial sounds

Discriminate among final sounds

## MATERIALS

Notebook or picture of a notebook, pictures from magazines and books showing objects that begin with *n* and other consonants

## BUILD BACKGROUND

- Display a notebook and have it identified.
- Have children listen as you say the words *notebook* and *nail*. Ask if the two words begin with the same sound. Have children repeat the words. Then, say the word *tent*, and ask if the word begins with the same sound as *notebook*.
- Say the following pairs of words. Have children nod once if both words begin with the same sound as *notebook*. Have children say the word *"no"* if they do not. Use these word pairs: *nest, newspaper; noodle, table; nap, car; needle, napkin; nut, nice; night, basket; neck, apple; neighbor, net.*

## DEVELOP/APPLY

### Use the Page

- Write the number 15 on the chalkboard. Ask children to turn to page 15 in their books.
- Direct children's attention to the key picture at the top of the page and have them identify it as a notebook. Then, invite children to look at the scene and make up a story about what they see. You may wish to suggest the following story starter: *It was noon and nice nurse Nancy was . . .* Encourage children to include the different items they see in the picture.
- Have children point to the nickel and tell why there is a line drawn around it. Ask them to say the words *notebook* and *nickel* and then trace over the line with a pencil.
- Have children complete the page by drawing a line around each picture whose name begins like *notebook*.

## REINFORCE

- Help children form groups of five to play a game called "Look and See." Explain that you will give each group member a picture, but they must not look at it. Tell children that three of the pictures show things that begin like *notebook* and the other two pictures show things that begin with other consonant sounds. At your signal, children hold up their pictures for the other members of their group to see. Each child then looks at the other pictures and guesses whether he or she is holding a picture of something that begins with *n*. When you say, "Look and see!" the children who think they have *n* pictures should hold them up above their heads. Children can then confirm their guesses.
- Challenge children to name nine words that begin with the same letter and sound as *notebook*. Children can use first names. Count aloud as children suggest words.
- Tell children that you will say some sentences. Explain that when they hear a word in the sentence that begins with /n/*n* they should raise their hands. Use these sentences:
  1. Nan has a new necklace.
  2. My neighbor's name is Ned.
  3. Nitza naps at night.
  4. Here are nine nails for a nickel.

## CHALLENGE

**Final Consonant:** /n/*n*
Say the following words and have children repeat each one after you: *fan, pin, hen, on, sun.* Ask how the words end. Then say the following sets of words:

| 1. pin | can | nail | 3. fin | net | pen |
| 2. nose | hen | sun | 4. nut | run | ran |

Have children say the two words that end with the /n/ sound. Challenge children to make up their sets of words.

# Initial Consonant: /n/*n*

DIRECTIONS: Help children identify the letters and pictures. Ask them to draw a line around the letter *n* in the word *notebook* and write *n* on the lines. Then in each box, have children write the letter *n* above each picture that begins with the same letter and sound as the key picture.

1. nail
2. scissors
3. nest
4. needle
5. newspaper
6. net
7. basketball
8. nurse

16

Initial Consonant: /n/*n*

## OBJECTIVES

Phonics and Decoding Skills

Recognize initial consonant: /n/*n*

Recognize final consonant: /n/*n*

## MATERIALS

ABC cards or letter cards for *N* and *n*, picture cards of objects beginning with *n* and other letters

## BUILD BACKGROUND

- Display letter cards for *N* and *n*. As you point to each letter, have children identify it as capital *N* and lowercase *n*. Say the word *notebook*. Elicit from children that the word begins with the letter *n*. Write the word on the chalkboard and ask a volunteer to underline the letter *n*.
- Provide children with letter *n* cards. Have them hold up the card when they hear you say a word that begins with /n/*n*. Use these words: *nut, card, newspaper, nail, turkey, noodle, car, needle, bowl, apple, napkin, nose.*

## DEVELOP/APPLY

### Use the Page
- Write the number 16 on the chalkboard, and have children turn to page 16 in their books.
- Ask children to point to the key picture and identify the letter that begins the word *notebook*. Have them draw a line around the letter *n*.
- Point to the letter *n* on the lines in the notebook and have children identify the *n*. Then have children write over the letter on the line, starting at the red dot. You may wish to demonstrate how to form the letter on the chalkboard. Then have children write *n*.
- Ask children to find the picture of the nail. Have them say *notebook* and *nail* and decide whether the two words begin with the same letter and sound. Point out the letter above the nail. Have children identify the letter as *n* and then write over it with a pencil.
- Invite children to identify the pictures in the remaining boxes and then write *n* above each picture that begins like *notebook*.

### Reading
Have children look for words in story books that begin with /n/*n*.

### Writing
Have children write in their Journals the *n* words they find.

## REINFORCE

- Clear an area in the classroom. Help children form pairs. Ask each pair to work together and arrange their bodies to form a lowercase *n*. Explain that they can lie down on the floor or stand and bend. Then challenge each group to name a word that begins with /n/*n*. List the words on the chalkboard. Have children say the words after you. Then ask volunteers to underline the *n*'s on the chalkboard.
- Draw a large notebook page on the chalkboard or on chart paper, or use an actual notebook. Remind children that the word *notebook* begins with the letter *n*. Tell children you will read some words aloud. Each time they hear a word that begins with *n*, have a volunteer write the letter *n* in the notebook. Use these words: *never, cart, nine, barrel, now, tag, number, carrot, name, hammer, not, noise, nothing.*
- Display picture cards showing objects whose names begin with /n/ and objects beginning with other letters. Call on volunteers to choose the pictures that begin like *notebook*.

## CHALLENGE

**Final Consonant:** /n/*n*
Have children listen for the /n/ in each of these words: *nap, ten; nail, pin; nut, hen; not, sun; nod, fin.* Say each word again and have children repeat the word that ends with /n/.

# Auditory Discrimination: /a/*a*

DIRECTIONS: Help children identify the key picture at the top of the page. Then have them draw a line around the pictures that begin with the same sound as the word *apple*. Have children think of other words that begin with the same sound as *apple*.

Auditory Discrimination: /a/*a*    Children should also circle alligator, ants, anchor, apple.                    17

## OBJECTIVES

Phonics and Decoding Skills

Discriminate among initial sounds

## MATERIALS

ABC cards or letter cards for *a*, an apple or picture of an apple, scissors, oaktag, marker, tape, radio or tape recorder and music cassette

- Ask children to answer this riddle: *What's red, green, or gold; juicy; and good to eat?* If children do not answer *apple*, display an apple or a picture of an apple.
- Have children listen as you say the words *apple* and *animal*. Ask if the two words begin with the same sound. Have children repeat the words. Then, say the word *banana* and ask if the word begins with the same sound as *apple*.
- Say the following pairs of words. Have children clap their hands once when both words begin with the same sound as *apple*. Use these word pairs: *apple, balloon; apple, ant; apple, table; apple, act; apple, nail; apple, carrot; apple, alphabet; apple, alligator.*

## DEVELOP/APPLY

### Use the Page
- Write the number 17 on the chalkboard and have children turn to page 17 in their books.
- Point to the key picture at the top of the page and have children identify it as an apple. Then, invite children to look at the picture and tell a story about the alligator and the ants. You may wish to suggest the following story starter: *One warm, sunny afternoon, Alligator decided to take a nap . . .* Encourage children to name the different things they see in the picture.
- Have children point to the ants. Ask why there is a line around the one ant. (*Ant* begins with the same sound as *apple*.) Have children say the words *apple* and *ant* and then trace over the line.
- Have children complete the page by drawing a line around each object whose name begins with the same sound as *apple*. Encourage children to suggest other words that begin with the same sound as *apple*.

- Cut out eight large circles from oaktag and write *a* on each. In an open space, tape the large circles to the floor. Ask children to pretend that the circles are rocks in a river, and in the river there are alligators, just like the one on page 17 in their books. Tell children that to cross the river safely, they can step from rock to rock, only when they hear a word that begins with the same sound as *apple*. Say words with initial /a/*a* and words with other initial sounds. Possible /a/*a* words: *at, an, and, as, ax, accident, acrobat, actor, add, adventure, after, alley, ambulance, anchor, angry, animal, ant, astronaut, ask, answer, attic.*
- Ask children to stand in place next to their desks. Play some music and invite them to wiggle or move their bodies in place. Explain that you will say some words. When they hear a word that begins with the same sound as *apple*, they must stop wiggling or moving and stand as still as statues. When you say a word that begins with a sound other than /a/, they can wiggle or move in place. Use these words: *ant, bear, cat, anchor, nail, table, alligator, car, bat, ax, telephone, am, cup, as, ashes, camera, box, astronaut, bug, tag, animal.* Continue with other words as needed.
- Distribute the letter cards for *a*. Read a paragraph from a favorite story or make up sentences with words that begin with the same sound as *apple*. Ask children to hold up their letter cards every time they hear a word that begins with the same sound as *apple*.

# Initial Vowel: /a/*a*

DIRECTIONS: Help children identify the letters and pictures. Ask them to draw a line around the letter *a* in the word *apple* and write *a* on the lines. Then in each box, have children write the letter *a* above each picture that begins with the same letter and sound as the key picture.

apple

1. alligator

2. ant

3. nickel

4. seven

5. animals

6. ax

7. footprint

8. astronaut

Macmillan/McGraw-Hill

18

Initial Vowel: /a/*a*

## OBJECTIVES

Phonics and Decoding Skills

Recognize initial vowel: /a/*a*

## MATERIALS

ABC card or letter card for *a*, drawing paper, crayons, red construction paper cutouts of apples, butcher paper, tape, markers, jump rope or ball, *Zoo-Be-Doo*

## BUILD BACKGROUND

- Display letter card for *a*. Point to the letter and have children identify it as an *a*. Review with children that the word *apple* begins with the letter *a*. Write the word *apple* on the chalkboard, and ask a volunteer to underline the letter *a*.
- Provide each child with a letter *a* card. Ask children to hold up their letter *a* cards when they hear you say a word that begins with the same letter and sound as *apple*. Use these words: *astronaut, bag, ask, animal, card, answer, tent, nickel, after, best, attic, ambulance, turkey.*

## DEVELOP/APPLY

### Use the Page
- Write the number 18 on the chalkboard and have children turn to page 18 in their books.
- Ask children to identify the key picture as *apple*. Have them point to the word *apple*, name the letter at the beginning of the word, and then draw a line around the *a*. Have children say the word *apple* aloud.
- Point to the letter *a* on the lines in the apple and have it identified as *a*. Then, have children write over the letter on the line, starting at the red dot. You may wish to demonstrate how to form the letter on the chalkboard. Then, have children practice writing the letter *a*.
- Have children point to the picture of the alligator. Ask them to say *apple* and *alligator* and then decide whether the two words begin with the same letter and sound. Point out the letter above the alligator. Have children identify the letter as a lowercase *a* and then write over the letter.
- Ask children to identify the remaining pictures in the boxes and then write *a* above each picture whose name begins with the same letter and sound as *apple*.

### Reading
Invite children to look through *Zoo-Be-Doo* and find words that begin with /a/*a*.

## REINFORCE

- Provide each child with drawing paper and crayons. Have children write the letter *a* at the top of their papers. Then, ask them to draw a picture of something whose name begins with the same letter and sound as *apple*. Invite children to share and talk about their pictures.
- Play "Pin the Apple on the Apple Tree" with the children. Cut out a supply of large, red construction paper apples. Draw an outline of a tree on butcher paper and have children color the trunk and branches brown and the leaves green. Tape the tree to the wall. Each child can tape or "pin" an apple on the tree by naming a word that begins with the same letter and sound as *apple*. As a word is suggested, help the child write it on the apple cutout and underline the letter *a*. Tell children they can use first names and the names of special places, as well as any other words they know.
- Teach children the following jump rope jingle: *A my name is Alice, and my brother's name is Al. We come from Atlanta, and we sell apples.* As children identify the words that begin with the same sound as *apple*, write them on the chalkboard.

Ask volunteers to underline the letter *a* in *Alice, Al, Atlanta, and,* and *apples.* Then, invite children to suggest other names for boys, girls, special places, and things to "sell" that begin with the same letter and sound as *apple*. List them on the chalkboard and have volunteers continue to underline each initial /a/*a*. Possible responses may include: *Ann, Abigail, Andrea, Allison, Alan, Adam, Andrew, Anthony, Alabama, Africa, Alaska, ants, alligators, animals.*

Then, ask volunteers to jump rope or bounce a ball as they say the jingle, using the different names, places, and things they suggested.

# Initial Consonants Review: /b/*b*, /k/*c*, /t/*t*,/n/*n*

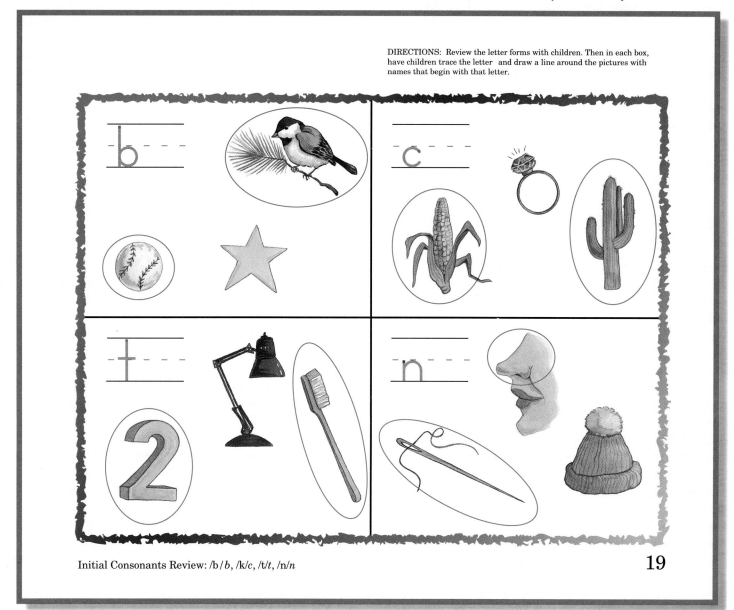

DIRECTIONS:  Review the letter forms with children. Then in each box, have children trace the letter  and draw a line around the pictures with names that begin with that letter.

Initial Consonants Review: /b/*b*, /k/*c*, /t/*t*, /n/*n*

19

## OBJECTIVES

Phonics and Decoding Skills

Recognize initial consonants: /b/*b*, /k/*c*, /t/*t*, /n/*n*

Recognize final consonants: /b/*b*, /t/*t*, /n/*n*

## MATERIALS

Letter cards for *b, c, t, n;* pictures of a box, cup, tent, and notebook; large oaktag circle; oaktag spinner; paper fastener; marker

- Display letter cards for *b, c, t,* and *n,* and ask children to identify the letters.
- Display pictures or illustrations for box, cup, tent, and notebook, and ask children to name the objects. Then have children name the letter that stands for the beginning sound in *box.* Call on a volunteer to hold up the picture for box and the letter card *b.* Continue the procedure for each picture and initial letter.
- Distribute letter cards *b, c, t,* and *n* to the children and invite them to listen as you say sets of three words. Have them repeat each word, hold up the letter card for the beginning sound, and then say the name of the letter. You may wish to use these words:

  **1.** bat, ball, balloon    **5.** bug, band, butter
  **2.** cat, car, comb    **6.** cake, candle, card
  **3.** top, table, tire    **7.** ten, toast, tape
  **4.** nut, nap, nickel    **8.** nap, note, name

## DEVELOP/APPLY

**Use the Page**
- Write the number 19 on the chalkboard, and have children turn to page 19 in their books.
- Direct children's attention to the first box on the left at the top of the page. Point to the letter and have children identify *b.* Tell children to write over the letter, starting at the red dot on the top line. Demonstrate how to form the letter *b* on the chalkboard, if necessary. Then, point to the pictures in the box and have children identify them. Ask children to draw a line around the pictures whose names begin with /b/*b* .
- In the box to the right, have children identify and write over the letter *c,* and then draw a line around the pictures whose names begin with /k/*c.*
- Continue this procedure with the letter *t* in the box on the bottom left and the letter *n* in the box on the bottom right.

- Cut a large circle from oaktag, divide it into fourths, and write one of the following letters in each part of the circle: *b, c, t,* and *n.* Next, cut out an oaktag spinner and attach it with a paper fastener. Then divide the class into teams. Have the players on each team take turns moving the spinner and saying a word that begins with the letter indicated by the spinner. List each team's words on the chalkboard. Continue the game until each player has had a chance to play. The team with the most words at the end of the game is the winner. You may wish to read each team's word list and have volunteers identify and underline the initial consonants.
- Play "Make a Match." Help children form groups of eight and then arrange themselves in a circle. Each group will need four pictures of things that begin with *b, c, t,* and *n,* and four corresponding letter cards. Use a different set of pictures for each group. As you randomly distribute pictures and letter cards to each group, tell children not to look. When each group is ready, say, "Make a Match." Have children look at their letters and pictures, identify them, and then match the letters with the pictures whose names begin with each letter. The group that correctly matches their letters and pictures first, wins the round. Collect the pictures and letter cards, give each group a new set, and then repeat the activity.

**Final Consonants Review:** /b/*b,* /t/*t,* /n/*n*
Distribute letter cards for *b, t,* and *n.* Tell children that you will say some words that end with /b/, /t/, and /n/. After you say each word, have children hold up the letter card that stands for the final sound. Use these words: *fan, tub, bat, ran, sit, sob, met, crib.*

# Listening, Speaking, Viewing

20

Listening, Speaking, Viewing

## OBJECTIVES

Listening, Speaking, Viewing Skills

Apply Comprehension Strategies in Viewing Activities

Compare and contrast

Tell a story about a picture

## MATERIALS

*Zoo-Be-Doo* Big Book; letter cards for *d, f, g, h, e;* postcard; markers or crayons; 5″ x 8″ blank index cards

- Reread the Big Book, *Zoo-Be-Doo,* inviting children to look for these animals: fox, dolphin, hippo, elephant, and gorilla. As you come to the places in the story where these animals appear, stop and talk about the animals and their environments.
- You might wish to begin a discussion about environments by asking these questions: *Where does the dolphin live? What other animals live in the water? Which animal lives in a rocky area near the tiger and the lion? How would you describe where the elephant lives? Why do you think a gorilla or a hippo might like this same area?*

## DEVELOP/APPLY

### Use the Page
- Write the number 20 on the chalkboard and say it aloud. Have children turn to page 20 in their books.
- Invite children to describe the scene by telling a story about the children and their visit to the zoo. Write these words on the chalkboard and have children repeat them after you: *gorilla, girl, hippo, hat, elephant, egg, dollar, dime, feather, feet.*
- Choose five pairs of children and give each pair a different letter card: *d, f, g, h,* or *e.* Instruct each pair to find two words on the chalkboard that begin with the letter on their card. When they find the words, direct them to draw a line around the letter.

### Writing
Point out the postcards at the souvenir stand on page 20. Display a postcard and explain how it is addressed and what is usually written on the back of the postcard. Discuss why people send postcards. Then invite pairs of children to work together to create their own postcards that tell about something they like at the zoo. Children may wish to take their postcards home to their families.

- Try some of these fun poems and rhymes. After reading them aloud, ask children to compare the animals in the poems to the real animals. Elicit how the two are alike and different.

"The Elephant Carries a Great Big Trunk" by an anonymous author and "Holding Hands" by Lenore M. Link (*Read-Aloud Rhymes for the Very Young* by Jim Trelease, Knopf, 1986).

"The Hippopotamus" by Jack Prelutsky (*Random House Book of Poetry for Children* by Jack Prelutsky, 1983).

- Have children walk like elephants, gorillas, and hippos. Ask them to think of words that describe each kind of walk. Conclude the activity by comparing the animals and the way they walk.

**Elephants:** children stretch their arms out in front of them and clasp hands like a trunk. As they take heavy steps, they swing their "trunks" back and forth.

**Gorillas:** children bend knees and bend slightly at the waist. They walk forward with their hands touching the ground.

**Hippos:** children walk on all fours with slow, heavy steps.

# Letter Identification: *D, F, G, H, E*

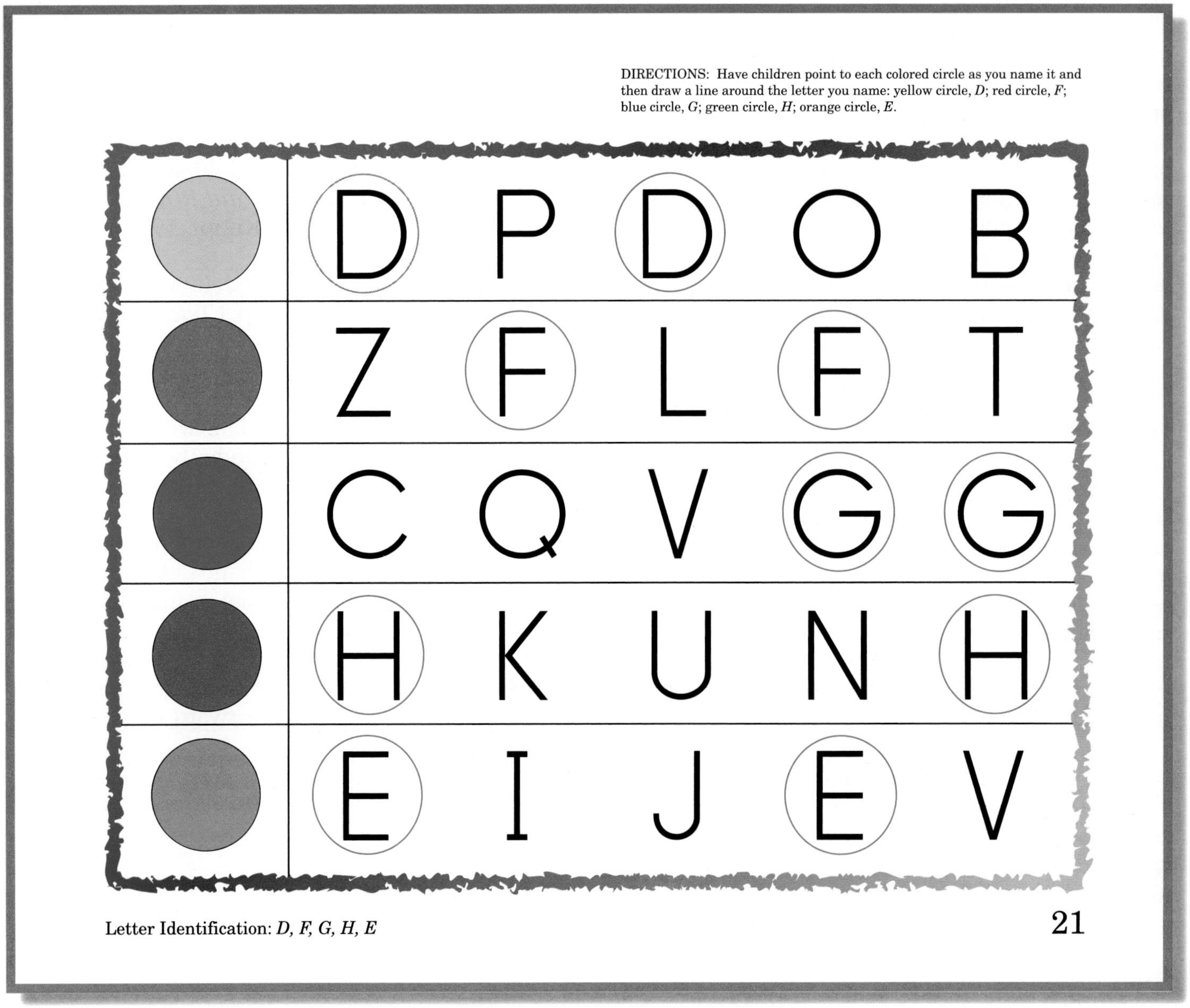

DIRECTIONS: Have children point to each colored circle as you name it and then draw a line around the letter you name: yellow circle, *D*; red circle, *F*; blue circle, *G*; green circle, *H*; orange circle, *E*.

| | | | | | | |
|---|---|---|---|---|---|---|
| ⬤ | D | P | D | O | B | |
| ⬤ | Z | F | L | F | T | |
| ⬤ | C | Q | V | G | G | |
| ⬤ | H | K | U | N | H | |
| ⬤ | E | I | J | E | V | |

Letter Identification: *D, F, G, H, E*

21

**OBJECTIVES**

Phonics and Decoding Skills

Identify capital letters: *D, F, G, H, E*

**MATERIALS**

ABC cards or letter cards for *D, F, G, H, E*; newspapers; red crayons

## BUILD BACKGROUND

- Display the front page of a newspaper and point to some of the capital letters that children have already learned, such as *B, C, T, N,* and *A.* Tell children that today they will be learning the names of more capital letters.
- Display the letter card for *D.* Ask children to name the letter. Continue with the remaining capital letters *F, G, H,* and *E.*
- Distribute one letter card, *D, F, G, H,* or *E,* to each child. Name one of the letters and ask the children who have that letter to hold up their cards and say the letter name aloud. Continue with the remaining letters.

## DEVELOP/APPLY

**Use the Page**
- Write the number 21 on the chalkboard and have children turn to page 21 in their books.
- Have children point to the yellow circle at the beginning of the first row and the letters that follow. Encourage them to name the letters they know. Point to the letter with the line around it. Have children identify it as capital *D* and write over the line. Then, ask children to find the other capital *D* in the row and draw a line around it, too.
- Have children point to the red circle and name the letters they know. Then, have them draw a line around each capital *F.*
- In the row with the blue circle, have children name the letters they know, and draw a line around each capital *G.*
- Continue with the two remaining rows for capital letters *H* and *E.*

## REINFORCE

- Display letter cards *D, F, G, H,* and *E* along the chalkboard ledge or on the bulletin board. Distribute a newspaper page and a red crayon to each child. Ask children to draw a line around the capital letters *D, F, G, H,* and *E* that they find in the headlines. Then, encourage them to share and compare the letters they circled and to tell how the letters are alike or different.
- Clear a large area in the classroom, or take children to the playground. Give each child one letter card, *D, F, G, H,* or *E.* Have children form a large circle. Call out capital letter *D.* Have all children with that letter step inside the circle to form a new circle. Then, have them march around once to the right, holding up their letter cards. Next, call out capital letter *F.* Have all children with that letter step inside the *D* circle to form a third circle. Then, have them march around once to the left, holding up their letter cards. Continue until there are five capital letter circles, each inside the other. At your signal, have each circle of children hold up their letter cards and march in alternating directions.
- Invite children to play "Stop and Go." Have them form groups of five and then sit on the floor in circles. Give each group a set of letter cards for *D, F, G, H,* and *E.* Have each child take a letter card and hold it face down. When you say *GO!* have children pass their letter cards to the children on their right. When you say *STOP!* have children turn over the cards and, in turn, name the letters they have. After identifying the letters, have them hold the cards face down and listen to your signals.

# Letter Identification: *d, f, g, h, e*

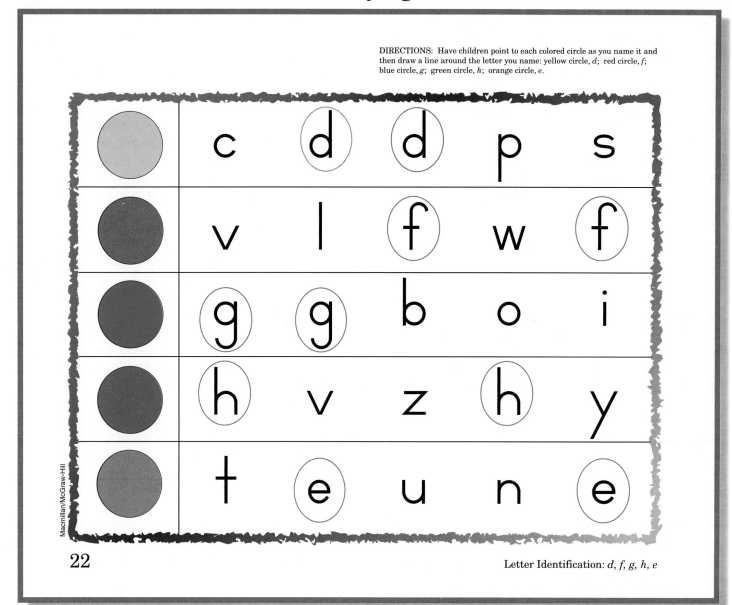

DIRECTIONS: Have children point to each colored circle as you name it and then draw a line around the letter you name: yellow circle, *d*; red circle, *f*; blue circle, *g*; green circle, *h*; orange circle, *e*.

| | | | | | |
|---|---|---|---|---|---|
| ● | c | ⓓ | ⓓ | p | s |
| ● | v | l | ⓕ | w | ⓕ |
| ● | ⓖ | ⓖ | b | o | i |
| ● | ⓗ | v | z | ⓗ | y |
| ● | t | ⓔ | u | n | ⓔ |

Macmillan/McGraw-Hill

22

Letter Identification: *d, f, g, h, e*

## OBJECTIVES

Phonics and Decoding Skills

Identify lowercase letters: *d, f, g, h, e*

## MATERIALS

ABC cards or letter cards for *D, F, G, H, E,  d, f, g, h, e*; marker; tape; chalk; large bag or pillowcase; cardboard; scissors; beanbags; sandpaper

**22** • **Letter Identification**: *d, f, g, h, e*

- As a review, display capital letter cards *D, F, G, H, E,* and have children identify them. Tell children that today they will be learning about lowercase letters *d, f, g, h,* and *e.*
- Display the letter card for lowercase *d.* Ask children to name the letter. Then, encourage them to look around the classroom for examples of lowercase *d.* Repeat with lowercase letters *f, g, h,* and *e.*
- Distribute one letter card *d, f, g, h,* or *e* to each child. Call on a volunteer to stand up and face the class, hold up the letter, and say the name of their letter card. Have all children who have that letter respond by holding up their cards and saying the name of the letter aloud.

## DEVELOP/APPLY

**Use the Page**
- Write the number 22 on the chalkboard and have children turn to page 22 in their books.
- Have children point to the yellow circle in the first row. Encourage them to name the letters they know. Point to the letter with the line around it. Have children identify it as lowercase *d* and write over the line. Then, ask children to find the other lowercase *d* and draw a line around it, too.
- Have children point to the red circle and name the letters they know. Then, have them draw a line around each lowercase *f.*
- In the row with the blue circle, have children name the letters they know and then draw a line around each lowercase *g.*
- Continue with the two remaining rows for lowercase letters *h* and *e.*

- Cut out five squares from cardboard. Write a different lowercase letter on each: *d, f, g, h,* and *e.* Tape each square to the floor and use chalk to mark a starting line a few feet away. Invite children to stand on the starting line and take turns throwing a beanbag on a square and then naming the letter. Allow each child three or four throws.
- Play the game "I Spy" with the children. Say, "I spy lowercase *d* on the (Job Chart). Who can find the letter?" Call on a volunteer to point to the letter on the chart. Continue in the same way with the other letters.
- Cut lowercase letters *d, f, g, h,* and *e* out of sandpaper. Make each letter about five inches high. Display the letters and have children identify them. Then, place the letters in a bag. Have children, in turn, close their eyes, reach into the bag with both hands for a letter, feel the shape of the letter, and then name the letter before taking it out of the bag to check. Children place the letter back into the bag after it is checked. Other letters that children have learned may be added to the bag as well.

As a variation, you may wish to name the letters you would like children to find.

# Auditory Discrimination: /d/*d*

DIRECTIONS: Help children identify the key picture at the top of the page. Then have them draw a line around the pictures that begin with the same sound as the word *door*. Have children think of other words that begin with the same sound as *door*.

Auditory Discrimination: /d/*d*

23

Children should also circle dinosaur, deer, duck, dog, desk, darts, dartboard.

## OBJECTIVES

Phonics and Decoding Skills

Discriminate among initial sounds

Discriminate among final sounds

## MATERIALS

Drawing paper, crayons, pictures or objects whose names begin with *d*

## BUILD BACKGROUND

- Pretend you are trying to unlock a door. Ask children to guess what you are doing. Invite children to guess how many doors there are on their floor in school. Record their guesses. Take children on a counting walk around the school at a later time to count the doors.
- Tell children to listen as you say the words *door* and *dog.* Ask if the two words begin with the same sound. Have children repeat the words. Then, say the words *door* and *cat*, and ask if the words begin with the same sound.
- Say the following pairs of words. Have children say the word in each pair that begins with the same sound as *door.* Use these word pairs: *doughnut, bug; cow, doll; dime, nickel; moon, danger; dollar, tent; baby, dishes.*

## DEVELOP/APPLY

**Use the Page**
- Write the number 23 on the chalkboard. Ask children to turn to page 23 in their books.
- Point to the key picture at the top of the page and have children identify it as a door. Then, invite children to tell a story about the four animal characters and the game they are playing. You may wish to prompt children with these questions: *What is Dinosaur doing? What is Duck pretending to be? Where are Dog and Deer trying to hide? What other game do you see?* Encourage children to include the different things they see in the picture in their story.
- Have children point to the darts. Ask why there is a line around the one dart. (*Dart* begins with the same sound as *door.*) Children then say *door* and *dart* and trace over the line.
- Have children complete the page by drawing a line around each thing that begins with the same sound as *door.* Encourage children to name other words that begin like *door.*

## REINFORCE

- Invite children to play "Who Says That?" To answer each question, have children name a person, animal, or object that begins like *door.* Encourage children to answer in complete sentences.
  **1.** What says, "Bow wow wow?" (dog)
  **2.** Who says, "Where does it hurt?" (doctor)
  **3.** What says, "Hee haw, hee haw?" (donkey)
  **4.** What goes, "Ding dong, ding dong?" (doorbell)
  **5.** Who says, "Do you brush and floss each day?" (dentist)
  **6.** What says, "Quack quack?" (duck)

  You may wish to place pictures of a dog, doctor, donkey, doorbell, dentist, and duck in different spots around the room. As children name the person, animal, or object, have them find the matching picture.
- Distribute a sheet of drawing paper and a crayon to each child. Show children how to draw a door on their papers. Then have them hold up their "door" each time they hear you say a word that begins like *door*. Use these words: *nice, dear, doll, boy, cat, dull, tune, donkey, cart, dinosaur, dent, bed.*

## CHALLENGE

**Final Consonant:** /d/*d*
Have children listen and then repeat each of the following words after you: *bed, sad, kid, nod, mud, paid, need, load.* Encourage children to tell how the words are alike. If necessary, tell them that all the words end with the sound of /d/. Then, as you say the following words, one at a time, have children clap once if the word begins with the sound of /d/ and stamp their feet once if it ends with the sound of /d/: *need, lid, dog, duck, head, date, road, said, dime.*

# Initial Consonant: /d/ *d*

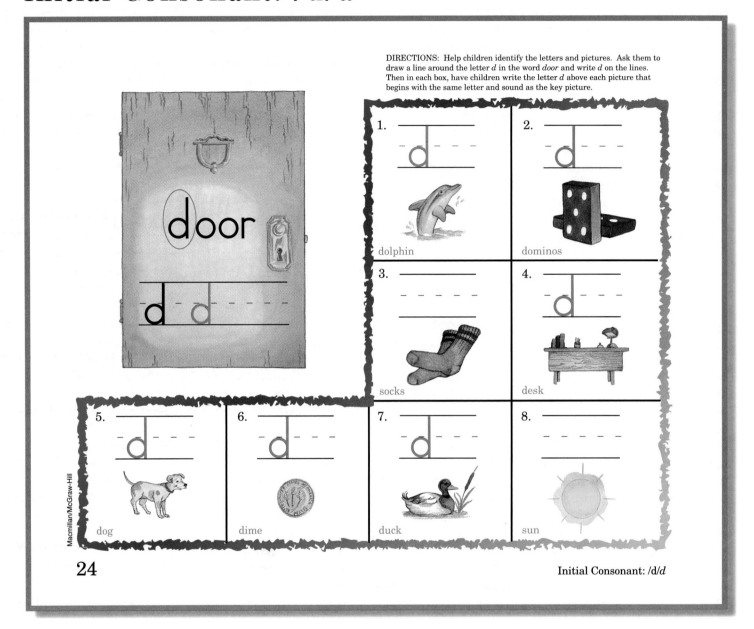

DIRECTIONS: Help children identify the letters and pictures. Ask them to draw a line around the letter *d* in the word *door* and write *d* on the lines. Then in each box, have children write the letter *d* above each picture that begins with the same letter and sound as the key picture.

door

1. dolphin
2. dominos
3. socks
4. desk
5. dog
6. dime
7. duck
8. sun

Macmillan/McGraw-Hill

24

Initial Consonant: /d/*d*

## OBJECTIVES

Phonics and Decoding Skills

Recognize initial consonant: /d/*d*

## MATERIALS

ABC cards or letter cards for *D* and *d*, picture cards whose names begin with *d* and other consonants, drawing paper, markers, crayons, blank word cards, tape

- Display letter cards *D* and *d.* As you point to each letter, have it identified as capital *D* or lowercase *d.* Write the word *door* on a large index card or oaktag strip, tape it to the classroom door, and then point to the letter *d.* Say the word aloud. Explain that *door* begins with the letter *d.*
- Distribute letter cards for *d* to the children. Ask them to hold up the letter card when they hear you say a word that begins with the same letter and sound as *door.* Use these words: *dog, button, daisy, dust, camera, night, dime, tent, dish, dictionary, baby.*

## DEVELOP/APPLY

**Use the Page**
- Write the number 24 on the chalkboard and say it aloud. Have children turn to page 24 in their books.
- Direct children's attention to the key picture. Ask children to name the letter at the beginning of *door,* and draw a line around it.
- Point to the letter *d* on the lines in the door. Ask children to identify lowercase *d,* and then write over the letter, starting at the red dot. Demonstrate the proper way to form the letter on the chalkboard. Then have children practice writing the letter *d.*
- Ask children to find and point to the picture of the dolphin. Have them say *door* and *dolphin.* Ask if the two words begin with the same letter and sound. Then point out the letter *d* above the dolphin. Have children write over the letter as they did in the key picture.
- Point out the remaining boxes and have children identify the picture in each one. Tell children to write *d* above each picture that begins with the same letter and sound as *door.*

- Distribute drawing paper and crayons to the children. Have them write lowercase *d,* and then use the letter to make a drawing of something that begins like *door.* When children have completed their drawings, help them write the word that names their picture. As children share their pictures, have them point out the letter *d* in their drawings and words.
- Invite children to brainstorm a list of words beginning with /d/*d* as in *door.* As each child suggests a word, help the child write it on a blank word card and then tape it to the classroom door. You may wish to write the letter *d* with a marker of one color and the remaining letters with a marker of another color. Afterward, invite children to come up to the door, point out and say the words they know.
- Display the picture cards for /d/*d* as well as other pictures in random order along the chalkboard ledge. Call on a volunteer to find a picture that begins like *door,* hold it up, and name it. Continue until all the *d* pictures have been identified.

**MEETING INDIVIDUAL NEEDS**

**Second-Language Support**
Some children may have difficulty discriminating between lowercase *d* and lowercase *b.* You might want to have children work in pairs to identify *d* and *b* as you display pairs of words.

# Auditory Discrimination: /f/ƒ

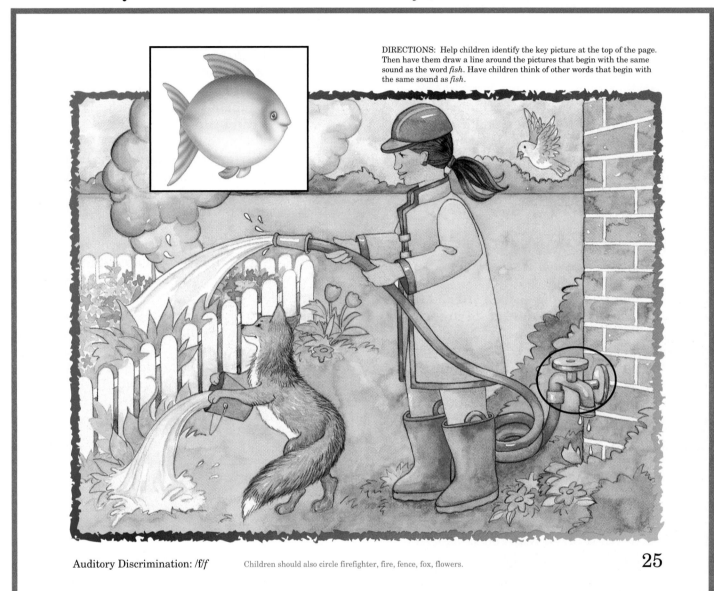

DIRECTIONS: Help children identify the key picture at the top of the page. Then have them draw a line around the pictures that begin with the same sound as the word *fish*. Have children think of other words that begin with the same sound as *fish*.

Auditory Discrimination: /f/ƒ    Children should also circle firefighter, fire, fence, fox, flowers.    25

## OBJECTIVES

Phonics and Decoding Skills

Discriminate among initial sounds

Discriminate among final sounds

## MATERIALS

Picture of a fish, pictures and objects whose names begin with /f/ƒ, **Sing a Sound Audiocassette**, Tape 1

## BUILD BACKGROUND

- Display a picture or illustration of a fish and have it identified. Tell children to listen as you say the words *fish* and *fox*. Ask if the two words begin with the same sound. Have children say the words aloud. Then, say the words *fish* and *dog*, and ask if the words begin with the same sound.
- Say the following pairs of words. Have children pretend to cast a fishing line when they hear two words beginning with the same sound as *fish*. You may wish to use these word pairs: *fun, fair; fat, hen; fox, finger; find, feather; dish, fork; face, fan; four, five; cat, find.*

## DEVELOP/APPLY

### Use the Page
- Write the number 25 on the chalkboard. Ask children to turn to page 25 in their books.
- Point to the key picture at the top of the page and have it identified as a fish. Then invite children to describe the scene. Have them describe what is on fire, how the fire might have started, who is helping to put out the fire, and where the water is coming from. Encourage children to include in their descriptions the different things they see in the picture.
- Have children point to the faucet and say the word aloud. Ask why there is a line drawn around the faucet. Children should recognize that *faucet* begins like *fish*. Have children trace over the line drawn around the faucet.
- Invite children to complete the page by drawing a line around each object whose name begins with the same sound as *fish*. Encourage children to name other words that begin like *fish*.

## REINFORCE

- Invite children to play "I'm Flying to Finland." Have the first child in a row begin by saying, "I'm flying to Finland and I'm bringing my ___" and then finish the sentence by naming something that begins like the word *fish*. Have the next child repeat what the first child said and then add something else that begins like *fish*. Have the children in the row continue in a similar manner until someone misses or cannot think of a word that begins like *fish*. Then begin again, this time at the end of the row.
- Give children one minute to walk around the room to find things that begin with /f/f. Arrange additional pictures, objects, and toy figures as needed beforehand. Have children return to their seats with the item or picture and then take turns telling what they found by saying, "Fe, Fi, Fo, Fum, I found a (fork to eat my food)." Ask the class to say the word *fork*, for example, as the child holds up the picture, object, or figure. Possible objects include toy fire engine, fish, fork, feather, funnel.
- Play the song "I've Been Workin' on the Railroad" on **Sing a Sound Audiocassette**, Tape 1, Side 2. Have children vary the *Fee, Fi Fiddlee-i-o* refrain by changing the vowels around, as in *Foo, Fay, Fodelee-ay-i.*

## CHALLENGE

### Final Consonant: /f/f
Have children listen and then say the words *fish* and *leaf*. Help them recognize that *fish* begins with /f/f and *leaf* ends with /f/f. Then, as you say the following words, one at a time, have children point to the front of the room if the word begins with /f/ and point to the back of the room if it ends with /f/. Use these words: *four, roof, fox, foal, calf, if, Frank, loaf, father, chef, half, farmer, fun, funny, thief, goof, famous, fire, chief.*

# Initial Consonant: /f/*f*

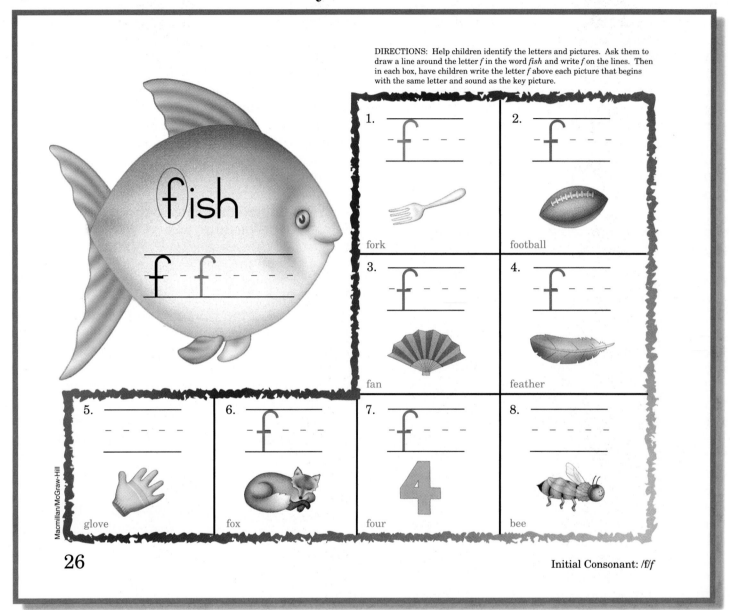

DIRECTIONS: Help children identify the letters and pictures. Ask them to draw a line around the letter *f* in the word *fish* and write *f* on the lines. Then in each box, have children write the letter *f* above each picture that begins with the same letter and sound as the key picture.

fish

f   f

1.   f   fork

2.   f   football

3.   f   fan

4.   f   feather

5.   glove

6.   f   fox

7.   f   four

8.   bee

Macmillan/McGraw-Hill

26

Initial Consonant: /f/*f*

## OBJECTIVES

Phonics and Decoding Skills

Recognize initial consonant: /f/*f*

Recognize final consonant: /f/*f*

## MATERIALS

ABC cards or letter cards for *F* and *f*, chart paper, construction paper, fish cutouts, scissors, paste, magazines, newspapers, tape, class experience stories

- Display the letter cards for *F* and *f*. Point to each letter and have it identified as capital *F* or lower-case *f*. Say the word *fish*. Tell children that it begins with the letter *f*. Write the word *fish* on the chalkboard and point to the letter *f*.
- Give each child a letter card for *f*. Ask them to hold up the letter card when they hear you say a word that begins with the same sound as *fish*. Use these words as needed: *father, tent, feet, funny, box, cup, five, notebook, fort*.

## DEVELOP/APPLY

### Use the Page
- Write the number 26 on the chalkboard. Have children turn to page 26 in their books.
- Direct children's attention to the key picture and have it identified as a fish. Ask children to name the letter at the beginning of *fish*, and draw a line around it.
- Point out the letter on the lines in the fish. Ask children to identify lowercase *f*. Invite them to write over the letter, starting at the red dot. You may wish to demonstrate how to form the letter on the chalkboard. Then have children practice writing *f*.
- Ask children to find and point to the picture of the fork. Have them say *fork* and *fish*. Ask if the two words begin with the same letter and sound. Then point out the letter *f* above the fork, and have children write over the letter as they did in the key picture.
- Have children identify the picture in each of the remaining boxes and then write *f* above each picture whose name begins like *fish*.

### Reading
Display class experience stories to groups of children and have them look for words that begin with /f/*f*. As each group reports the words it found, list them on the chalkboard and have children read them aloud with you.

- Draw a large outline of a fish tank or fishbowl on chart paper and display it on a bulletin board. Cut out fish outlines from construction paper. Then distribute the fish cutouts, scissors, paste, magazines, and newspapers to the children. Have them cut out words that begin with *f* and paste them on their fish cutouts. Invite children to read their words aloud. Children, in turn, can then tape their fish in the fish tank or fishbowl on the bulletin board.
- Write the following sentences on the chalkboard and read each one aloud:
  **1.** Fuzzy Fox found four forks.
  **2.** Firefighters fight fires.
  **3.** Felix fixed five fish for Fanny.

Encourage children to note that each word begins with /f/*f*. Have volunteers underline the letter *f* in each word. Then challenge children to take turns saying each sentence five times as quickly as they can. You may wish to have children make up and dictate their own sentences using *f* words.

### Final Consonant: /f/*f*
Write the words *leaf* and *calf* on the chalkboard and say each word aloud. Ask children to identify the sound they hear at the end of each word and the letter that stands for that sound. Have volunteers underline the final *f* in each word. Then read aloud the following sentences:
**1.** I ate half a sandwich.
**2.** We baked a loaf of bread.
**3.** Dad made beef with noodles.
**4.** A thief stole the woman's purse.
**5.** Our cat climbed onto the roof.
**6.** My sister wants to be a chef.

Challenge children to identify the word that ends in /f/*f*. Write the word on the chalkboard.

## Auditory Discrimination: /g/g

DIRECTIONS: Help children identify the key picture at the top of the page. Then have them draw a line around the pictures that begin with the same sound as the word *gate*. Have children think of other words that begin with the same sound as *gate*.

Auditory Discrimination: /g/g     Children should also circle gorilla, girl, goat, garbage can, green hat, grass.

27

**OBJECTIVES**

Phonics and Decoding Skills

Discriminate among initial sounds

Discriminate among final sounds

**MATERIALS**

Picture or illustration of a gate, **Sing a Sound Audiocassette**, Tape 1

- Display a picture or illustration of a gate and have children identify it. Then invite children to tell where they have seen gates.
- Have children listen as you say the words *gate* and *goat*. Ask if the two words begin with the same sound. Have children say the words aloud. Then say the words *gate* and *cat*, and ask if the words begin with the same sound.
- Say the following pairs of words. Have children raise both hands if the words begin with the same sound as *gate*. Have them raise one hand if only one word in the pair begins with the same sound as *gate*. Use these word pairs: *good, garden; goat, donkey; guppy, goose; garage, gift; gorilla, tiger; guitar, gold*.

## DEVELOP/APPLY

**Use the Page**
- Write the number 27 on the chalkboard. Have children turn to page 27 in their books.
- Direct children's attention to the key picture at the top of the page and have it identified as a gate. Then invite children to look at the picture and tell a story about the gorilla, girl, and goat. You may wish to suggest a story starter such as the following: "*Gorilla, Goat, and Gail had nothing to do, so they decided to . . .*" Encourage children to include the different things they see in the picture in their story.
- Have children point to the guitar and tell why there is a line around it. (*Guitar* begins with the same sound as the key picture *gate*.) Have children say *gate* and *guitar* and then trace over the line with a pencil.
- Have children complete the page by drawing a line around each object whose name begins with the same sound as *gate*. Then encourage children to think of other words that begin like *gate*.

- Invite children to march around the room as you say words slowly. Explain that when they hear a word that begins with the same sound as *gate*, they are to freeze (stop marching). They can march again when you say "March." Use these words and others: *girl, go, gone, get, game, garage, got, give*.
- Brainstorm a list of *g* words with the children. Then say the following sentences and have children identify the words that begin like *gate: Gordon has a goose. Gail has a gown.* Invite children to take turns adding other *g* words to each sentence, such as: *Gordon and Gilda have a golden goose and a guitar*. Names and words children may use are: *Goldie, Gilda, Godfrey, Gomer, gorilla, gum, guitar, goat, good, gold, goofy, gorgeous*.
- Play the traditional English song "The Green Grass Grows All Around" (**Sing a Sound Audiocassette**, Tape 1, Side 2). Encourage children to substitute other words that begin with the sound /g/ for *green grass*.

**Final Consonant:** /g/g
As you say the following words, have children repeat each one after you: *rag, pig, fog, leg, mug*. Ask how the words are alike. Help children recognize that all the words end with /g/. Then say the following sets of words:

| | | |
|---|---|---|
| goat | gorilla | hog |
| bag | game | go |
| geese | wig | guitar |
| hug | gallop | garden |

Have children say the one word in each set that ends with /g/. Then challenge children to make their own sets of words.

# Initial Consonant: /g/g

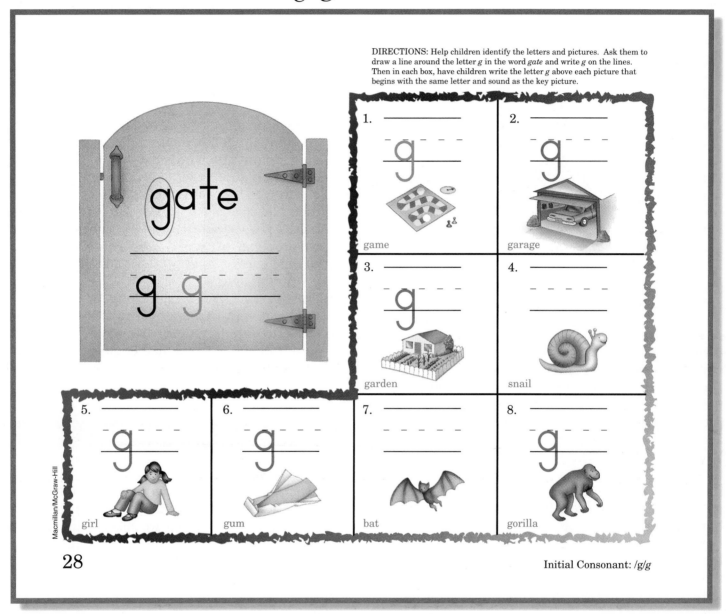

DIRECTIONS: Help children identify the letters and pictures. Ask them to draw a line around the letter *g* in the word *gate* and write *g* on the lines. Then in each box, have children write the letter *g* above each picture that begins with the same letter and sound as the key picture.

gate

g g

1. ____
g
game

2. ____
g
garage

3. ____
g
garden

4. ____
snail

5. ____
g
girl

6. ____
g
gum

7. ____
bat

8. ____
g
gorilla

Macmillan/McGraw-Hill

28

Initial Consonant: /g/g

## OBJECTIVES

Phonics and Decoding Skills

Recognize initial consonant: /g/g

Recognize final consonant: /g/g

## MATERIALS

ABC cards or letter cards for *G* and *g*, storybooks, butcher paper, crayons, construction paper flower cutouts, tape, pipe cleaners, newspapers, drawing paper

## ACTIVITIES — BUILD BACKGROUND

- Display the letter cards for *G* and *g*. As you point to the letters, have children identify the capital *G* and lowercase *g*. Say the word *gate*. Tell children that it begins with the letter *g*. Write the word *gate* on the chalkboard and point to the letter *g*.
- Give each child a letter card for *g*. Tell them to hold up the card each time they hear you say a word that begins with the same letter and sound as *gate*. Use these words: *girl, gum, balloon, cupcake, good-bye, telephone, gold, gas*. Encourage children to name additional words that begin with the same letter and sound as *gate*.

## DEVELOP/APPLY

### Use the Page
- Write the number 28 on the chalkboard. Have children turn to page 28 in their books.
- Ask children to point to the key picture and identify it as a gate. Then ask children to name the letter at the beginning of *gate,* and draw a line around it.
- Point to the letter on the lines in the *gate.* Have children identify lowercase *g*, and then write over the letter, starting at the red dot. Then have children practice writing *g*.
- Ask children to find and point to the picture of the game. Have them say *gate* and *game*, and tell whether both words begin with the same letter and sound. Then point out the letter *g* above the game, and have children write over the letter as they did in the key picture.
- Have children identify the pictures in the remaining boxes. Have them write *g* above each picture whose name begins with the same letter and sound as *gate*.

### Reading
Ask children to look through books to find and read words that begin with /g/*g*.

## ACTIVITIES — REINFORCE

- Decorate a bulletin board with butcher paper. Cut out flowers from construction paper. Draw a garden plot with rows of stems. Invite children, in turn, to name a word that begins like *gate,* and write each word on a paper flower cutout. Help children tape their flowers to the stems in the garden.
- Provide children with one pipe cleaner each. Have them shape the pipe cleaner into a lowercase *g*. Then distribute drawing paper and crayons. Have children trace over their pipe cleaner letter to form a row of *g*'s.
- Help children form groups. Provide each with a page of newspaper and crayons. Ask each group to find as many words as they can that begin with *g*. Invite the groups to show their newspaper pages and say any words they know.

## ACTIVITIES — CHALLENGE

**Final consonant:** /g/*g*
Say the words *get* and *bug* as you write them on the chalkboard. Ask a volunteer to underline the *g* in each word. Ask children to name other words that rhyme with *bug*. Have volunteers write the words on the chalkboard. Possible words are: *dug, hug, mug, rug, tug*. Call on other volunteers to draw a line under each word.

Then write the following sentence on the chalkboard and read it aloud: *I dug for worms in the garden.* Ask children to draw a line under the word that ends with /g/*g*. Follow a similar procedure with these sentences:
1. I gave my mom a hug.
2. Dad got a mug of tea.
3. I see gum on the rug.
4. Don't tug the goat.

# Auditory Discrimination: /h/*h*

DIRECTIONS: Help children identify the key picture at the top of the page. Then have them draw a line around the pictures that begin with the same sound as the word *hat*. Have children think of other words that begin with the same sound as *hat*.

Auditory Discrimination: /h/*h*     Children should also circle hippo, horse, house, hammer, heart, hose.

29

## OBJECTIVES

Phonics and Decoding Skills

Discriminate among initial sounds

Discriminate among final sounds

## MATERIALS

Different kinds of hats or pictures of hats; picture cards: harp, hat, house, donkey, feather, girl; magazine pictures of other objects whose names begin with /h/*h*; **Sing a Sound Audiocassette**, Tape 2

- Display different kinds of hats or pictures of hats. Talk about why people wear hats. Then invite children to describe the hats they wear, or would like to wear.
- Say the words *hat* and *house* and have children repeat the words after you. Ask if the two words begin with the same sound. Then say the words *hat* and *coat* and ask if the words begin with the same sound.
- Say the following pairs of words. Have children clap if both words in the pair begin with the same sound as *hat*. Use these word pairs: *hat, heart; hat, dog; hat, hand; hat, helicopter; hat, fish; hat, goat; hat, honey; hat, nickel.*

## DEVELOP/APPLY

### Use the Page
- Write the number 29 on the chalkboard. Have children turn to page 29 in their books.
- Have children point to the key picture and identify it as a hat. Then direct children's attention to the scene. Have the animals identified (hippo, horse, hamster) and ask children to tell where they are, what they are each doing, and what they are using. You may wish to have children tell a story about the picture.
- Say *hamster* and *hat*. Have children identify the beginning sound and letter in each word and ask why there is a line around the hamster. Then have children write over it.
- Invite children to complete the page by drawing a line around each object whose name begins with the same sound as *hat*. Encourage children to think of other words that begin like *hat*.

- Invite children to listen to the following sentences and then say the words they hear that have the same beginning sound as *hat*. Tell children that each sentence has two words with /h/. After children identify the two words, have them repeat the sentence. Use these sentences:
  **1.** I hear a harp.
  **2.** I hit my thumb with a hammer.
  **3.** My Uncle Harry plays the horn.
  **4.** My horse eats oats and hay.

  You may wish to have children make up their own sentences with words that begin with the same sound as *hat*.
- Place picture cards of the harp, hat, house, donkey, girl, and feather in a hat. Use additional magazine pictures of objects whose names begin with /h/ and other consonant sounds. Ask a volunteer to randomly pick a card from the hat, identify the picture, and show it to the class. Have the class then decide whether it begins with the same sound as *hat*. If the picture shows something that begins with /h/, have the child place it on the chalkboard ledge. If it does not, have the child put the card aside. Continue until all the pictures have been identified.
- Read or tell the story "The Three Little Pigs." Then help children form two groups: pigs and wolves. Tell the wolves to knock and say "Little, pig, little pig, let me in!" Tell the pigs to respond by saying, "Not by the hair on my chinny, chin, chin." Then have the wolves reply, "Then I'll huff and I'll puff and blow your house in." Tell children to emphasize each *h* word they say. Have the pigs and wolves then switch parts and dramatize the scene again.
- Play the African American playsong "Hambone" on **Sing a Sound Audiocassette**, Tape 2, Side 1, to provide additional practice with the /h/ sound. Have children substitute other /h/ words, such as *hamster* or *hippo*, for *hambone*.

# Initial Consonant: /h/*h*

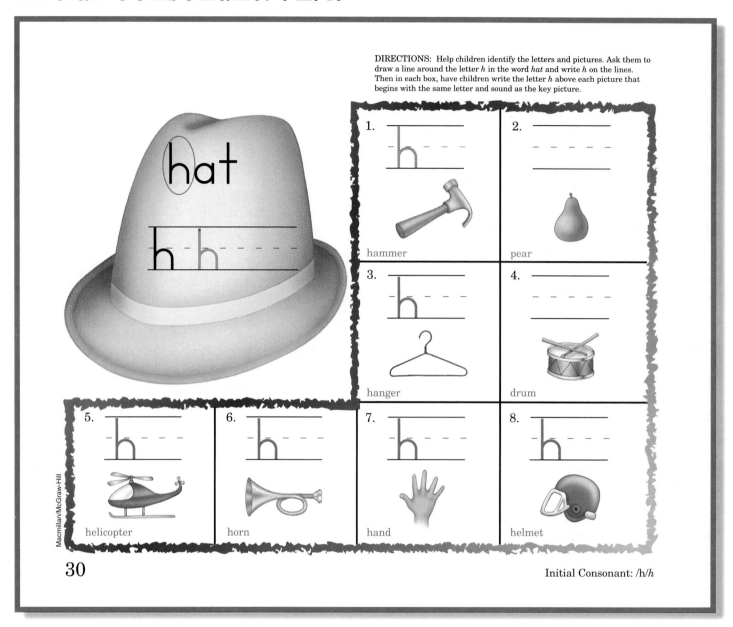

DIRECTIONS: Help children identify the letters and pictures. Ask them to draw a line around the letter *h* in the word *hat* and write *h* on the lines. Then in each box, have children write the letter *h* above each picture that begins with the same letter and sound as the key picture.

hat

1. hammer

2. pear

3. hanger

4. drum

5. helicopter

6. horn

7. hand

8. helmet

Macmillan/McGraw-Hill

30

Initial Consonant: /h/*h*

## OBJECTIVES

Phonics and Decoding Skills

Recognize initial consonant: /h/*h*

## MATERIALS

ABC cards or letter cards for *H* and *h*, fingerpaint paper, fingerpaints, scissors, paste, magazines, sentence strips, index cards

- Display the letter cards for *H* and *h*. As you point to each letter, in turn, have children identify it as capital *H* or lowercase *h*. Say the word *hat*. Elicit from children that *hat* begins with the letter *h*. Write *hat* on the chalkboard and point to the letter *h*.
- Give each child a letter card for *h*. Have children stand. Tell them to hold up the card and hop on one foot when they hear you say a word that begins with the same sound as *hat*. Use these words: *hand, foot, heart, finger, leg, head, heel, nose, hip*.

## DEVELOP/APPLY

**Use the Page**
- Write the number 30 on the chalkboard. Have children turn to page 30 in their books.
- Direct children's attention to the key picture and have them identify the *hat*. Then ask children to name the letter at the beginning of *hat*, and draw a line around it.
- Have children identify lowercase *h* on the lines inside the hat and then write over the letter, starting at the red dot. You may wish to demonstrate how to form the letter on the chalkboard. Then have children practice writing *h*.
- Ask children to find the picture of the hammer. Have them say *hat* and *hammer*. Ask if the two words begin with the same letter and sound. Point out the letter *h* above the hammer and have children write over the letter as they did in the key picture.
- Help children identify the remaining pictures. Tell them to write *h* above each picture whose name begins with the same letter and sound as *hat*.

- Distribute fingerpaints and fingerpaint paper to the children. Have them practice writing *h* using the paints. Then call on volunteers to hold up their papers and name a word that begins with *h*.
- Distribute magazines and scissors to the children. Have each child find and cut out a picture of something whose name begins with /h/*h*. Then, have each child hold up the picture, say the *h* word, and then make up a sentence using the word. Write the sentence on a sentence strip and have the child underline the word. Then display the pictures and sentence strips on the bulletin board.
- Make sets of word cards for *h* words and other previously learned consonants. Possible *h* words: *hat, ham, hot, hut, hen, has*. Give each group a set of word cards. Ask children to work together to make up a story using their words. Then have each group share its story with the rest of the class.

# Auditory Discrimination: /e/e

DIRECTIONS: Help children identify the key picture at the top of the page. Then have them draw a line around the pictures that begin with the same sound as the word *egg*. Have children think of other words that begin with the same sound as *egg*.

Auditory Discrimination: /e/e    Children should also circle elf, elephant, elevator, escalator.    31

## OBJECTIVES

Phonics and Decoding Skills

Discriminate among initial sounds

## MATERIALS

An egg or picture of an egg, picture cards and magazine pictures of objects whose names begin with /e/e, plastic egg or small ball

- Ask children to answer this riddle: *What comes in a shell and can be soft boiled, scrambled, or fried?* If children do not answer *egg*, display an egg or a picture of an egg.
- Say the words *egg* and *elephant* and have children repeat the words after you. Ask if the two words begin with the same sound. Then say the words *egg* and *apple* and ask if the words begin with the same sound.
- Say the following pairs of words. Have children call out "egg" if both words in the pair begin with the same sound as *egg*. Use these word pairs: *engine, elbow; elephant, ant; elevator, exit; empty, alligator; end, ice; enter, ever; elbow, elves.*

## DEVELOP/APPLY

### Use the Page

- Write the number 31 on the chalkboard. Have children turn to page 31 in their books.
- Have children point to the key picture and identify it as an egg. Then direct children's attention to the scene and invite children to tell a story about what they see. You may wish to provide this story starter: *"Elephant and Elf have been shopping. Elf bought . . ."*
- Direct children's attention to Elf's bag in the picture. Ask why there is a line around the Eskimo doll. (*Eskimo* begins with the same sound as *egg*.) Have children say both words and listen for /e/. Then ask children to write over the line.
- Invite children to complete the page by drawing a line around each object whose name begins with the same sound as *egg*. Encourage children to think of other words that begin like *egg*.

- Have children form a circle to play "Hot Boiled Eggs." Choose one child to be "It" and give him or her a plastic egg or ball. "It" passes the hot boiled egg to the child to his/her right. Tell children to pretend that it is a hot boiled egg so they should pass it around the circle as quickly as possible. When the child who is "It" calls out "hot boiled egg," the child who is holding the "egg" must say a word that begins with the same beginning sound as *egg*. Children can take turns being "It."
- Read aloud the following sentences. Have children repeat the words they hear that begin with the same sound as *egg*. Use these sentences:
  1. Ed and Edna rode an elephant.
  2. Elvis went up the down escalator.
  3. The elevator was empty.
  4. Have you ever seen an elf?
  5. I put the envelope on the end table.
- Hide the picture cards of objects whose names begin with /e/e as in egg. You may wish to cut out and hide additional pictures from magazines illustrating /e/e words. Then invite pairs of children to look for one of the picture cards. As they look, tell them whether they are getting *warm, warmer, hot, hotter, cool, cold, colder,* and so on. When children find the card, have them say the word aloud.

**MEETING INDIVIDUAL NEEDS**

**Second-Language Support**
You might wish to pair native English speakers with non-native English speakers to find the pictures hidden around the room.

# Initial Vowel: /e/*e*

DIRECTIONS: Help children identify the letters and pictures. Ask them to draw a line around the letter *e* in the word *egg* and write *e* on the lines. Then in each box, have children write the letter *e* above each picture that begins with the same letter and sound as the key picture.

egg

e   e

1. elephant

2. banana

3. elevator

4. stairs

5. exercise

6. escalator

7. butterfly

8. elf

Macmillan/McGraw-Hill

32

Initial Vowel: /e/*e*

## OBJECTIVES

Phonics and Decoding Skills

Recognize initial vowel: /e/*e*

Recognize medial vowel: /e/*e*

## MATERIALS

ABC cards or letter cards for *E* and *e*, drawing paper, crayons, construction paper egg shapes

- Display the letter cards *E* and *e*. As you point to each letter, have children identify the capital *E* and lowercase *e*. Say the word *egg*. Elicit that *egg* begins with the letter *e*. Write *egg* on the chalkboard and point to the letter *e*.
- Invite children to look through their books to find the letter *e*. Then provide children with letter *e* cards. Have children hold up their letter *e* cards when they hear you say a word that begins with the same sound as *egg*. Use these words: *elephant, otter, apple, elk, umbrella, exit, enter, ink, envelope, extra.* Encourage children to name other words that begin with the same sound as *egg*.

## DEVELOP/APPLY

### Use the Page

- Write the number 32 on the chalkboard. Have children turn to page 32 in their books.
- Direct children's attention to the key picture and have it identified. Point to the word *egg* and have children say it after you. Have children then point to the first letter of *egg*, say the letter name and its sound, and then draw a line around the letter *e*.
- Point to the letter *e* on the lines in the egg and have children identify it as lowercase *e*. Then have children write over the letter on the line, starting at the red dot. You may wish to demonstrate how to form the letter on the chalkboard. Then have children practice writing the letter *e*.
- Ask children to find the picture of the elephant. Have them say the words *egg* and *elephant*. Ask if the two words begin with the same letter and sound. Point out the letter *e* above the elephant and have children write over the letter.
- Help children identify the remaining pictures. Tell them to write *e* above each picture whose name begins with the same letter and sound as *egg*.

- Provide children with drawing paper and crayons. Have them write the letter *e* at the top of their papers; then ask them to draw a picture of something that begins with the same sound and letter as *egg*. Help children label their pictures. Invite volunteers to show and tell about their pictures.
- Brainstorm with the children a list of words and names that begin with the same sound as *egg*, and write them on the chalkboard. Distribute egg cutouts to the children and have them copy one word onto their egg. Collect the eggs and display them along the chalkboard ledge. Call out a word and have a child find the correct egg, hold it up, and say the word aloud.
- Teach children the following rhyme:

*Elizabeth, Elspeth, Eddie, and Bess,*
*They all went together to seek a bird's nest.*
*They found a bird's nest with eight eggs in,*
*They all took one, and left four in.*

Have children identify the /e/e words in the rhyme and then suggest other names that begin with /e/e that can be substituted for *Elizabeth, Elspeth,* and *Eddie.* Possible responses may include: *Edna, Elvis, Elvira, Elsie, Ellen, Emily, Eric, Erica, Elmo, Elliot, Esther,* and *Eleanor.*

### Medial vowel: /e/e

As you say the following words, have children repeat each one after you: *hen, bed, get, web, let, peg, hem, pep.* Ask children to identify the sound they hear in the middle of each word. Then say the words *elf, elk, elephant, exit, end, exercise, elevator, empty* and have the beginning sounds identified. Explain to children that /e/e can be heard at the beginning of words or in the middle of words.

# Initial Consonants Review: /d/*d*, /f/*f*, /g/*g*, /h/*h*

DIRECTIONS: Review the letter forms with children. Then in each box, have children trace the letter and draw a line around the pictures with names that begin with that letter.

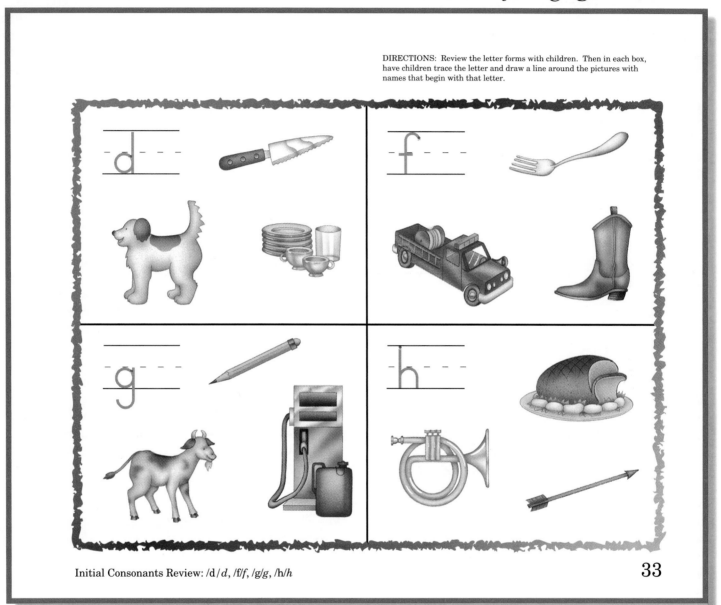

Initial Consonants Review: /d/*d*, /f/*f*, /g/*g*, /h/*h*

33

## OBJECTIVES

Phonics and Decoding Skills

Recognize initial consonants: /d/*d*, /f/*f*, /g/*g*, /h/*h*

Recognize final consonants: /d/*d*, /f/*f*, /g/*g*

## MATERIALS

Letter cards for *Dd, Ff, Gg, Hh;* picture cards of a door, fish, game, and hat; tape or chalk; index cards; cassette or CD with music

- Display the letter cards for *D, d, F, f, G, g, H,* and *h* and ask children to identify the letters as capital or lowercase.
- Display picture cards or illustrations for *door, fish, game,* and *hat* and have them identified. Call on volunteers to name the beginning sound and letter of each picture name.
- Distribute letter cards *d, f, g,* and *h* to the children. Invite them to listen as you say sets of three words. Have children repeat each word, hold up the letter card for the beginning sound, and then say the letter. You may wish to use these words.

  **1.** dolphin, domino, dime    **5.** desk, dog, duck
  **2.** feather, fox, four    **6.** fan, football, fork
  **3.** garden, gum, garage    **7.** gum, gorilla, goat
  **4.** hand, heart, head    **8.** hanger, horn, helmet

## DEVELOP/APPLY

**Use the Page**

- Write the number 33 on the chalkboard, identify it, and then have children turn to page 33 in their books.
- Direct attention to the first box on the left at the top of the page. Point to the letter and have children identify *d*. Have children write over the letter, starting at the red dot on the line. Demonstrate how to form the letter *d* on the chalkboard, if necessary. Then point to the pictures in the box and have them identified. Ask children to draw a line around the pictures whose names begin with /d/*d*.
- In the box to the right, have children identify and write over the letter *f.* Then point to the pictures in the box and have them identified. Ask children to draw a line around the pictures whose names begin with /f/*f.*
- Continue this procedure with the remaining boxes for letters *g* and *h.*

 REINFORCE

- Draw or tape a starting line and a finishing line on the floor. Use chalk to draw four large "stepping stones" between the two lines and then write one of these letters on each stepping stone: *d, f, g,* or *h.* Invite children to take turns hopping from one stepping stone to the next, saying a word that begins with the same letter and sound that appears on each stone. You may wish to add stepping stones for previously learned consonants.
- Assemble picture cards and letter cards for *d, f, g,* and *h.* Mix them up and have children work in small groups to match each picture to the letter that stands for the beginning sound heard in its name.
- Make a set of word cards whose words begin with the letters *d, f, g,* and *h.* Invite children to play a variation of musical chairs. Using one chair for each child, place a word card on each chair. Have children march around the chairs to music. When the music stops, have each child pick up the word on the closest chair, sit down, and identify the word and the letter that begins the word.

## CHALLENGE

**Final Consonants:** /d/*d*, /f/*f*, /g/*g*
Distribute letter cards for *d, f,* and *g* to the children. As you read aloud the following sets of words, have children hold up the letter card that identifies the final consonant of the words in each set. Use these words:

**1.** roof, loaf, chef
**2.** bed, sad, kid
**3.** rag, pig, fog
**4.** thief, if, leaf
**5.** nod, mud, pad
**6.** leg, mug, bug

Continue by writing some of the words on the chalkboard, omitting the final consonant. As you say the words, call on volunteers to identify and write the final consonant.

# Listening, Speaking, Viewing

34

Listening, Speaking, Viewing

## OBJECTIVES

Listening, Speaking, Viewing Skills

Apply Comprehension Strategies
in Viewing Activities

Identify picture details

Identify sequence

Recall details

## MATERIALS

*Zoo-Be-Doo* Little Books; chart paper;
letter cards for *j, m, p, l,* and *o;* paper
plates; yarn; markers; posterboard;
props to make animal costumes
(optional)

## ACTIVITIES — BUILD BACKGROUND

- Distribute individual copies of *Zoo-Be-Doo.* Reread the story, inviting children to join in.
- Invite children to imitate farm animals and household pets. Have the class guess the animal.
- When you finish reading the story, ask children what question was asked over and over again by the zookeeper. Ask children to recall the answer given by all the animals. Then copy the pattern on the chalkboard:

  The _____ did not know.
  The _____ did not know.
  "_____" said the
  _____.
  The _____ definitely did not know.

- Have children write a new part for the book. Instruct them to substitute new animals and animal sounds into the pattern. Record their sentences on chart paper, and read the new story part with the children.

## DEVELOP/APPLY

### Use the Page
- Write the number 34 on the chalkboard and say it aloud. Have children turn to page 34 in their books.
- Invite children to tell what is happening in the picture. Allow children who have been in a play or seen a live play to share their experiences. Elicit information about characters, costumes, props, audience, and how the story was presented.

### Writing
- Invite children to present a play. Have children decide which they would do first, next, and last. Have them decide on a familiar fairy tale or animal story to present. Then, in small groups, have them make a sign to advertise the play. The sign should include the name of the play and an illustration about the play.

## ACTIVITIES — REINFORCE

- Set out paper plates, yarn, markers, and other art supplies. Encourage children to use the materials to make a mask for each character in the play they plan to perform.
- Allow children time to rehearse. Then invite children to present their play to the class. Encourage the audience to tell the performers what they liked about the presentation.
- List on the chalkboard the names of the animals on page 34 and the names of each animal character in the play. Ask children to look at the beginning letter of each word and to sort the words according to their initial letter. Use children's responses to create lists on the chalkboard. Then have children match the letter cards *j, m, p, l,* and *o* to the words that begin with that letter.

# Letter Identification: *J, M, P, L, O*

DIRECTIONS: Have children point to each colored circle as you name it and then draw a line around the letter you name: yellow circle, *J*; red circle, *M*; blue circle, *P*; green circle, *L*; orange circle, *O*.

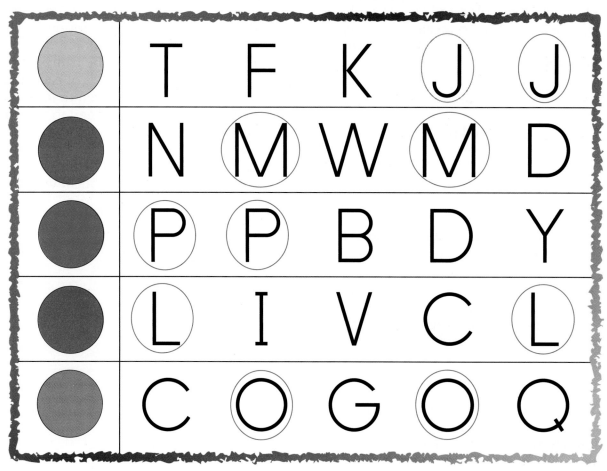

Letter Identification: *J, M, P, L, O*

35

## OBJECTIVES

Phonics and Decoding Skills

Identify capital letters: *J, M, P, L, O*

## MATERIALS

ABC cards or letter cards for *J, M, P, L, O;* drawing paper; marker; picture books; front pages of newspapers; paper; crayons

- Invite children to look at class charts, bulletin board displays, newpaper headlines, and book titles to find examples of the capital letters they have already learned: *B, C, T, N, A, D, F, G, H,* and *E.* Tell children that today they will be learning the names of more capital letters.
- Hold up the letter card for *J* and ask if anyone can name this letter. If children do not know, say that it is capital *J.* Then encourage children to look for words that begin with capital *J.* Follow a similar procedure to introduce capital letters *M, P, L,* and *O.*
- Distribute letter cards *J, M, P, L,* and *O,* one to each child. Write one of the letters on the chalkboard. Ask children who have the same letter card to stand up, show their letter, and then say the letter name aloud. Follow a similar procedure for the remaining letters.

## DEVELOP/APPLY

**Use the Page**
- Write the number 35 on the chalkboard and have children turn to page 35 in their books.
- Direct attention to the yellow circle at the beginning of the first row and have children name the letters they know.
- Ask children to name the letter in the first row that has a line around it (capital *J*). Then have children draw a line around each capital *J* in the row.
- Have children point to the red circle in the second row and name the letters they know. Then have them draw a line around each capital *M.*
- In the row with the blue circle, have children name the letters they know and draw a line around each capital *P.*
- Continue in this way with the two remaining rows for capital letters *L* and *O.*

- Help children form groups of five. Direct each group to a spot in the classroom and have them sit in a line on the floor. Distribute letter cards *J, M, P, L,* and *O,* one to each child in a group. Invite children to follow these directions:
  **1.** If you have capital letter *J,* stand up and face your group.
  **2.** If you have capital letter *M,* stand behind capital letter *J.*
  **3.** If you have capital letter *P,* stand in front of capital letter *J.*
  **4.** If you have a capital letter *L,* stand to the right of capital letter *J.*
  **5.** If you have capital letter *O,* stand to the left of capital letter *J.*
- Assign each pair of children a capital letter card: *J, M, P, L,* and *O,* and have them say the letter name aloud. Then give each pair a picture book or the front page of a newspaper, a crayon, and paper. Have children look for their assigned capital letter and keep a tally of the letters they find.
- Distribute drawing paper to each child. Assign each child a capital letter and have him/her practice writing that letter. Display children's work on a bulletin board.

**Second-Language Support**
Some children may have difficulty discriminating between capital letters *M, W,* and *N.* Have children work in pairs to practice tracing letter cards for each letter, talking about differences between the letters, and then looking at words beginning with these letters.

# Letter Identification: *j, m, p, l, o*

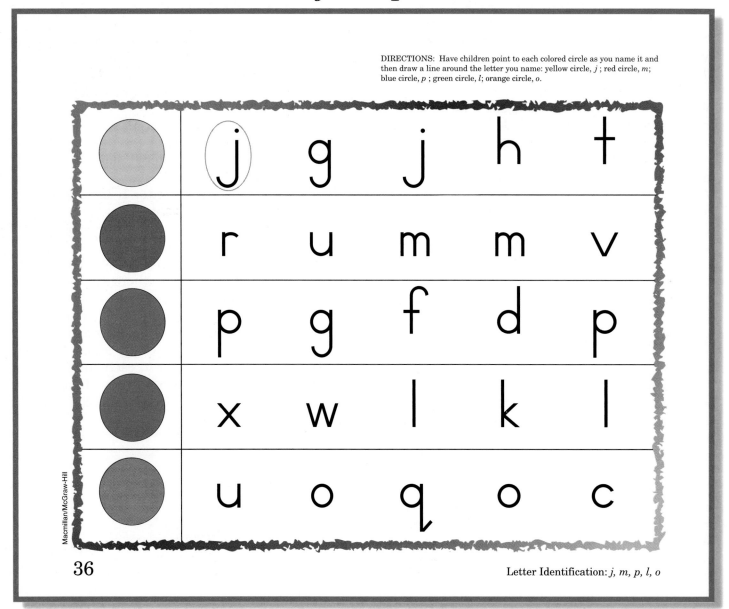

DIRECTIONS: Have children point to each colored circle as you name it and then draw a line around the letter you name: yellow circle, *j* ; red circle, *m*; blue circle, *p* ; green circle, *l*; orange circle, *o*.

Macmillan/McGraw-Hill

36

Letter Identification: *j, m, p, l, o*

## OBJECTIVES

Phonics and Decoding Skills

Identify lowercase letters: *j, m, p, l, o*

## MATERIALS

ABC cards or letter cards for *J, j, M, m, P, p, L, l, O, o;* cardboard or oaktag; markers; tape; beanbag

- Display capital letter cards *J, M, P, L,* and *O* and have them identified. Tell children that they will be learning about lowercase letters *j, m, p, l,* and *o.*
- Display the letter card for lowercase *j* and ask children to name the letter. Then write the following sentence on the chalkboard or on chart paper and read it aloud: *"I just drank a jug of juice."* Have volunteers point to and underline each letter *j.* Repeat the procedure with lowercase letters *m, p, l,* and *o.* Use these sentences:

  **1.** My mother made meatballs and spaghetti.
  **2.** We picked peaches and pears.
  **3.** The line in the lunchroom was long.

- Distribute letter cards for *j, m, p, l,* and *o,* so that each child has one card. Name one of the letters. Ask children who have that letter card to hold it up and say the name of the letter aloud. Continue the procedure with the remaining letters.

## DEVELOP/APPLY

**Use the Page**
- Write the number 36 on the chalkboard. Have children turn to page 36 in their books.
- Have children point to the yellow circle at the beginning of the first row. Invite children to name the letters they know. Then ask children to name the letter in the first row that has a line around it (lowercase *j*). Have children draw a line around the other lowercase *j* in the row.
- Next, ask children to point to the red circle in the second row and name the letters they know. Then have children draw a line around each lowercase *m.*
- In the row with the blue circle, have children name the letters they know and then draw a line around each lowercase *p.*
- Continue in a similar manner with the two remaining rows for lowercase letters *l* and *o.*

- Play "I Spy" with the children. Say, "I spy lowercase *p* on the bulletin board. Who can find that letter?" Call on a volunteer to point to the letter. Continue with other letters.
- Display the letter cards for *J, j, M, m, P, p, L, l,* and *O, o* on the chalkboard ledge and have them identified. Then write sets of letters such as the following on the chalkboard:

| 1 | | 2 | |
|---|---|---|---|
| J | p | M | l |
| M | l | P | o |
| P | o | O | m |
| L | m | L | j |
| O | j | J | p |

As you call out a letter, ask a child to draw a line to match the lowercase letter to the capital letter.
- Cut out large circles from oaktag. In each circle, write a lowercase letter and tape it to the floor. Have children stand behind a designated starting line and then take turns tossing a beanbag into a circle and naming the letter.

# Auditory Discrimination: /j/*j*

DIRECTIONS: Help children identify the key picture at the top of the page. Then have them draw a line around the pictures that begin with the same sound as the word *jar*. Have children think of other words that begin with the same sound as *jar*.

Auditory Discrimination: /j/*j*    Children should also circle jaguar, jacket, jacks, jug.    37

## OBJECTIVES

Phonics and Decoding Skills

Discriminate among initial sounds

## MATERIALS

Jar or picture of a jar; large, wide-mouth plastic jar; picture cards and magazine pictures of objects whose names begin with /j/*j* and other consonant sounds; **Sing a Sound Audiocassette**, Tape 2

- Display a jar or a picture of a jar and have it identified. Encourage children to name some things that come in jars.
- Have children listen as you say the words *jar* and *jam*. Ask if the two words begin with the same sound. Have children say the words aloud. Then, say the words *jar* and *game,* and ask if the words begin with the same sound.
- Say the following pairs of words. Have children clap if both words begin with the same sound as *jar*. Use these word pairs: *jar, jam; jar, garden; jar, tent; jar, fish; jar, junk; jar, jug; jar, hat; jar, jacket*.

## DEVELOP/APPLY

**Use the Page**
- Write the number 37 on the chalkboard. Have children turn to page 37 in their books.
- Direct children's attention to the key picture at the top of the page and have it identified. Then invite children to look at the picture and tell a story about the jaguar and the raccoon. You may wish to suggest a story starter such as the following: "*Jake Jaguar and Robin Raccoon are making a. . . .*" Encourage children to include the different things they see in the picture in their story.
- Have children point to the jack and tell why there is a line around it. (*Jack* begins with the same sound as the key picture *jar*.) Have children say *jar* and *jack* and then write over the line with a pencil.
- Have children complete the page by drawing a line around each object whose name begins with the same sound as *jar*. Then encourage children to think of other words that begin like *jar*.

- Place a large, wide-mouth plastic jar on a table, or make a large outline of a jar on the bulletin board. Place a variety of picture cards and magazine pictures of objects whose names begin with /j/j and the other consonant sounds face down on a table. Invite children to help you fill the jar with pictures whose names begin with the same sound as *jar*. Have children take turns selecting a card, saying the picture name, and then telling whether it begins with the same sound as *jar*. Children can then put the /j/j picture into the jar (or tape it onto the picture of the jar).
- Invite children to stand. Explain that you will read aloud several sentences, and whenever they hear you say a word that begins with the same sound as *jar*, they are to jump in place one time. Use these sentences:
  **1.** I watched Jan and Jackie jump rope.
  **2.** Janet helped James open the jar of jelly.
  **3.** In July we took a jumbo jet to Jacksonville.
  **4.** Jennifer bought new jeans and a jacket.

  Encourage children to make up their own sentences.
- Say the nursery rhyme "Jack and Jill." Ask children to identify the names that begin with the same sound as *jar*. Then invite children to suggest other names that begin with /j/j to substitute in the rhyme. Possible names are: *Jan, Jean, Joan, Jenna, Jacqueline, Joanne, Joe, Jim, Jeff, John, Justin*.
- Play the song "Jig Along Home" by Woody Guthrie, found on the **Sing a Sound Audiocassette**, Tape 2, Side 1. Encourage children to repeat the words to the song, clapping whenever they hear /j/j. Then have children substitute *jig* for other words such as *juggle, jump, jiggle,* and *jog*.

# Initial Consonant: /j/j

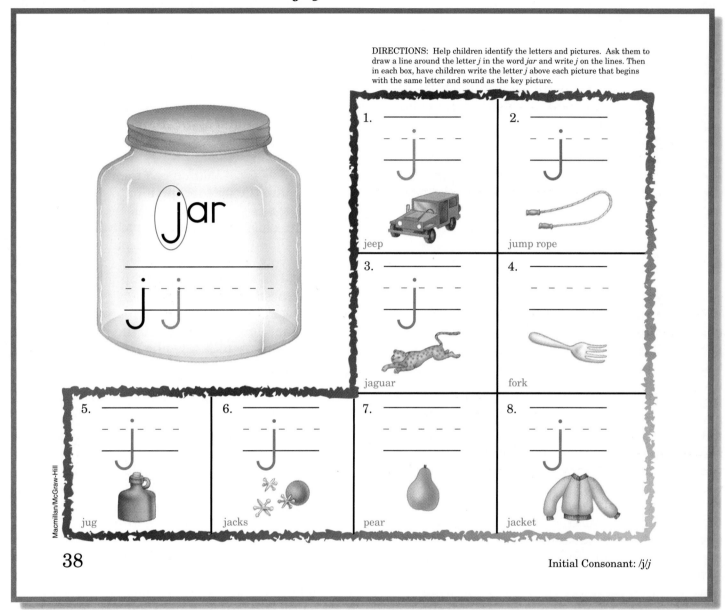

DIRECTIONS: Help children identify the letters and pictures. Ask them to draw a line around the letter *j* in the word *jar* and write *j* on the lines. Then in each box, have children write the letter *j* above each picture that begins with the same letter and sound as the key picture.

jar

1. ___ jeep

2. ___ jump rope

3. ___ jaguar

4. ___ fork

5. ___ jug

6. ___ jacks

7. ___ pear

8. ___ jacket

Macmillan/McGraw-Hill

38

Initial Consonant: /j/j

## OBJECTIVES

Phonics and Decoding Skills

Recognize initial consonant: /j/j

## MATERIALS

ABC cards or letter cards for *J* and *j*; large, wide-mouth jar; index cards; storybooks; magazines; paste; drawing paper; yarn

- Direct children's attention to the picture on page 37. Invite children to name some things that begin with the letter *j*. Write the letters *J* and *j* on the chalkboard.
- Display the letter cards for *J* and *j*. As you point to each letter in turn, have children identify it as capital *J* or lowercase *j*. Write the word *jar* on the chalkboard and have children say it with you. Elicit that the word *jar* begins with the letter *j*. Ask a volunteer to underline the letter *j*.
- Give each child a letter card for *j*. Ask children to hold up the letter card when they hear you say a word that begins with the same letter and sound as *jar*. Use these words: *jacket, monkey, pen, junk, juice, lamp, octopus, jewel, Jack, ostrich.*

### Use the Page

- Write the number 38 on the chalkboard and say it aloud. Have children turn to page 38 in their books.
- Direct children's attention to the key picture and have it identified. Have children point to the word *jar* and say it aloud. Then ask children to name the letter at the beginning of the word *jar* and draw a line around it.
- Point to the letter *j* on the lines in the *jar* and have children identify the lowercase *j*. Then have children write over the letter, starting at the red dot. If necessary, demonstrate the proper way to form the letter on the chalkboard. Then have children practice writing *j*.
- Ask children to point to the picture of the *jeep*. Have them say *jar* and *jeep*. Ask if the two words begin with the same letter and sound. Then point out the letter *j* above the *jeep* and have children write over the letter as they did in the key picture.
- Point out the remaining boxes and ask children to identify the picture in each one. Have children then write *j* above each picture that begins with the same sound and letter as *jar*.

- Invite children to play "I'm Thinking of Something." Ask children to think of something whose name begins with /j/*j* as in *jar*; then give clues for the class to guess. Use the following as a model: *I'm thinking of a short coat that keeps me warm* (jacket). As children guess each /j/*j* word, call on a volunteer to write the word on the chalkboard and underline the letter *j*. When you have compiled a list of words, read the list with the class.
- Place a large, wide-mouth jar on the table. Give each child several blank index cards, a story book, and a pencil or marker. Invite children to look for words they know that begin with the same sound as *jar*, and then print the words on the cards. Next have children read aloud the words before putting them in the jar. When the /j/*j* word jar is filled, encourage children to pick words out of it, say them aloud, and make up sentences.
- Provide children with yarn, scissors, paste, and drawing paper. Have children make a lowercase *j*, and paste their letter onto drawing paper. Then have children draw or cut out and paste magazine pictures of things that begin with the letter *j*. Invite children to share their letters and pictures with the class.

# Auditory Discrimination: /m/m

DIRECTIONS: Help children identify the key picture at the top of the page. Then have them draw a line around the pictures that begin with the same sound as the word *mitten*. Have children think of other words that begin with the same sound as *mitten*.

Auditory Discrimination: /m/m    Children should also circle monkey, mop, mail, mailbox, mouse.

39

## OBJECTIVES

Phonics and Decoding Skills

Discriminate among initial sounds

Discriminate among final sounds

## MATERIALS

Real mittens or picture of mittens, pictures of animals whose names begin with /m/m as well as other letters, **Sing a Sound Audiocassette,** Tape 2

- Put on a pair of mittens, or show a picture of some mittens. Have children identify the article of clothing. Invite them to describe the kind of weather in which mittens might be worn. Children may want to share winter experiences in which mittens kept their hands warm.
- Say the words *mitten* and *melt.* Ask if the words begin with the same sound. Then say the word *sun* and ask if it begins like *mitten.*
- Ask children to put on real or make-believe mittens and rub them together if both words in the pair begin with the same sound: *mitten, make; mile, map; mix, sled; muff, cold; money, milk; more, muffin; merry, ice.*

## DEVELOP/APPLY

### Use the Page
- Write the number 39 on the chalkboard and say it aloud. Have children turn to page 39 in their books.
- Direct children's attention to the key picture. Invite children to describe the scene on the page by telling a story about the monkey and the mouse.
- Point to the moon and have children identify it. Ask why the moon has a line drawn around it. (*Moon* begins with the same sound as *mitten.*) Have children say *mitten* and *moon* and then write over the line with a pencil.
- Encourage children to complete the page by drawing a line around each object whose name begins with the same sound as *mitten.* Ask children to name other words that begin with the same sound as *mitten.*

- Play a version of "Mother, May I." Select a child to play the part of the Mother. Other children line up across the room. Children, in turn, may take one giant step toward Mother if they end the question with a word that begins like *mitten. Mother, may I move? Mother, may I mop?* You may wish to brainstorm a list of words children could use in their questions before starting the activity: *milk, melt, mind, mumble, do magic, make a mess, mix.*
- Children will have fun creating their own version of the familiar folk tale "The Mitten," in which many animals crowd inside the same mitten to get out of the cold. Invite children to collect pictures of animals. As they retell the story, have only those animals whose names begin with the same sound as *mitten* make their home in the mitten. Then ask children to tell what happens when too many animals squeeze together in the mitten.
- As an additional activity, invite children to listen to the song "The Muffin Man" on the **Sing a Sound Audiocassette,** Tape 2, Side 2. You might also have them illustrate the song by drawing their favorite kind of muffin.

**CHALLENGE**

### Final Consonant: /m/*m*
Say the following words and have children repeat each one after you: *gum, ham, gym, mom, stem.* Ask how the words are alike. Help children recognize that all the words end with /m/. Challenge children to think of words that rhyme with *ham.* Point out that all of the rhyming words end with the same sound. Then use the rhyming words to make a two-line rhyme or poem.

# Initial Consonant: /m/*m*

DIRECTIONS: Help children identify the letters and pictures. Ask them to draw a line around the letter *m* in the word *mitten* and write *m* on the lines. Then in each box, have children write the letter *m* above each picture that begins with the same letter and sound as the key picture.

mitten

m  m

1. mask
2. moon
3. mailbox
4. stamp
5. monkey
6. marker
7. money
8. puzzle

Macmillan/McGraw-Hill

40

Initial Consonant: /m/*m*

## OBJECTIVES

Phonics and Decoding Skills

Recognize initial consonant: /m/*m*

Recognize final consonant: /m/*m*

## MATERIALS

ABC cards or letter cards for *M* and *m*, drawing paper, picture cards or objects whose names begin with /m/*m* and other consonants, paint or crayons, magazines, paste, scissors

- Display the letter cards *M* and *m*. As you point to each letter in turn, encourage volunteers to identify each as capital *M* or lowercase *m*. Say the word *mitten*. Explain that *mitten* begins with the letter *m*. Write the word *mitten*. Have a volunteer write over the letter *m*.
- Ask children to identify which of these words begins with the same sound as *mitten*: *move* or *stop*. Invite children to give a "thumbs-up" sign when they hear you say a word that begins with the same sound as *mitten*. Use these words: *machine, monkey, train, merry-go-round, march, dance, mosquito, kangaroo.*

## DEVELOP/APPLY

### Use the Page
- Write the number 40 on the chalkboard and say it aloud. Have children turn to page 40 in their books.
- Direct children's attention to the key picture. Ask them to identify the letter that begins the word *mitten* and then draw a line around the letter *m*.
- Point to the letter *m* on the lines in the mitten. Have children identify the lowercase *m*. Invite them to write over the letter, starting at the red dot. You may wish to demonstrate the proper way to form the letter on the chalkboard. Then have children practice writing the letter *m*.
- Ask children to point to the picture of the mask. Have them say *mitten* and *mask*. Ask if the two words begin with the same letter and sound. Then point out the letter *m* above the mask, and have children write over the letter as they did in the key picture.
- Point out the remaining boxes and challenge children to identify the picture in each one. Explain that they will write *m* above each picture whose name begins with the same letter and sound as *mitten*.

### Reading
Have children look for words that begin with /m/*m* in a favorite storybook or fairy tale.

- Distribute drawing paper to the children. Have them write or paint *m* on their paper, and then write one word that begins with the same letter and sound as *mitten*.
- Play a game called "Monuments." Explain that a monument, like a statue, cannot move. Have children walk around the room and freeze in a pose when you say "Freeze." They must stay in that pose until you show a picture whose name begins with /m/*m*. Then they may walk around and strike a new pose when you say "Freeze" again.
- Invite children to create an "M Collage." Have them look through magazines to find words that begin with *m*. Have children cut out the words and arrange them in an interesting design on chart paper to create a collage. Display children's work.

## CHALLENGE

**Final Consonant:** /m/*m*
Have children listen for the ending sound as you say these names of people: *Sam, Tim, Tom, Kim,* and *Pam.* Ask children what they notice about the end of each name. (It ends with /m/*m*.) Add children's names that end with *m* to the list.

# Auditory Discrimination: /p/*p*

DIRECTIONS: Help children identify the key picture at the top of the page. Then have them draw a line around the pictures that begin with the same sound as the word *pillow*. Have children think of other words that begin with the same sound as *pillow*.

Auditory Discrimination: /p/*p*    Children should also circle pants, pumpkin, pickles, pineapple, pie.    41

## OBJECTIVES

Phonics and Decoding Skills

Discriminate among initial sounds

Discriminate among final sounds

## MATERIALS

Small pillow or picture of a pillow; picture cards for *map, harp, jeep, up, lamp, fan,* and *sock;* **Sing a Sound Audiocassette,** Tape 2

- Pantomime fluffing a pillow and putting it under your head. Pretend to go to sleep. Ask children to guess the object you are using (pillow). Display a real pillow or show a picture of one. Ask children to share words that describe how a pillow feels.
- Say the word *pillow* emphasizing the beginning sound. Then say *pillow* and *pajamas* and ask children if the words begin with the same sound. Say the word *bed* and ask if it begins like *pillow*.
- Read the pairs of words. Ask children to pretend to rest their heads on a pillow if both words begin with the same sound as pillow: *pink, pants; pan, pitcher; panda, koala; pancakes, bacon; puppet, parrot; purple, green; push, pull; puppy, piglet.*

## DEVELOP/APPLY

### Use the Page
- Write the number 41 on the chalkboard and say it aloud. Have children turn to page 41 in their books.
- Direct children's attention to the key picture at the top of the page and have it identified. Explain that the animals and people in the picture are at a county fair. Invite children to tell a story about the fair using the picture clues on the page. Encourage them to look for details in the picture that show what is being judged.
- Point to the pig that is about to get a prize and have children identify it. Ask why the pig has a line drawn around it. (*Pig* begins with the same sound as *pillow*.) Have children say *pillow* and *pig* and then write over the line with a pencil.
- Encourage children to complete the page by drawing a line around each object whose name begins with the same sound as *pillow.* Ask children to name other words that begin with the same sound as *pillow*.

- Play "Pass the Pillow." Have children sit in a circle and pass a small pillow around the circle. When you say "Stop," the person holding the pillow says a word that begins with the same sound as *pillow*.
- Sing the nursery rhyme "Pease Porridge Hot" with the children. Ask children to listen for words that begin like *pillow.* Write the words to the rhyme on the chalkboard. Have children underline each word that has the same beginning sound as the key word.

**Pease Porridge Hot**

Pease porridge hot,
Pease porridge cold,
Pease porridge in the pot,
Nine days old.

- Develop a list of words that begin with /p/*p* with the children (*peach, pillow, picture, pen, pail, pear, pin*). Then call on volunteers to pantomime a word. Have the rest of the class guess the word that is being pantomimed.
- Have children listen to the song "Pawpaw Patch," on the **Sing a Sound Audiocassette,** Tape 2, Side 2. After they are familiar with the song, invite children to substitute their own *p* words for *pawpaw.* To get them started, you might suggest *pickle, pepper,* and *pineapple.*

**Final Consonant:** /p/*p*
Display picture cards for *map* and *harp.* Have children say the name of each picture. Point out that both end with the same sound. Have children repeat these words after you, listening for the ending sound: *cup, mop, zip, lap, leap, nap.* Display the picture cards *jeep, up, lamp, fan,* and *sock.* Have children sort the pictures into two piles: words that end with the same sound as *map* and words that do not.

# Initial Consonant: /p/*p*

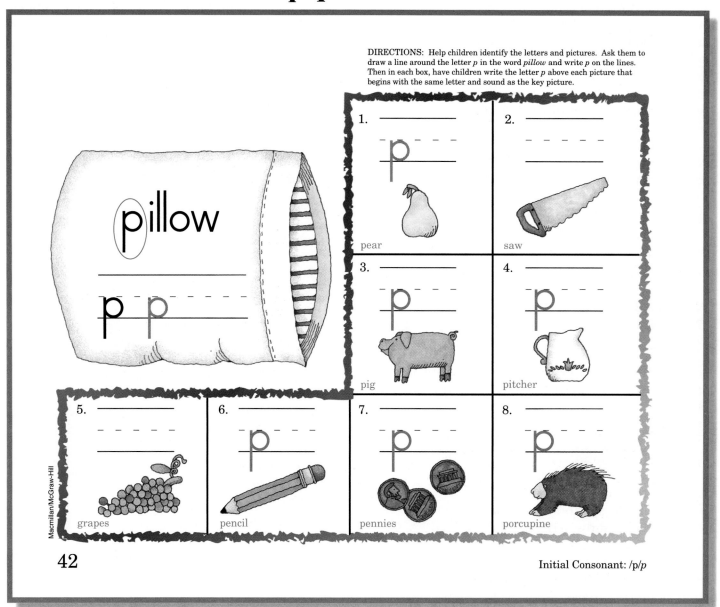

DIRECTIONS: Help children identify the letters and pictures. Ask them to draw a line around the letter *p* in the word *pillow* and write *p* on the lines. Then in each box, have children write the letter *p* above each picture that begins with the same letter and sound as the key picture.

pillow

p p

1. _____  pear

2. _____  saw

3. _____  pig

4. _____  pitcher

5. _____  grapes

6. _____  pencil

7. _____  pennies

8. _____  porcupine

Macmillan/McGraw-Hill

42

Initial Consonant: /p/*p*

## OBJECTIVES

Phonics and Decoding Skills

Recognize initial consonant: /p/*p*

Recognize final consonant: /p/*p*

## MATERIALS

ABC cards or letter cards for *P* and *p*, chalk, drawing paper, crayons, magazines, scissors, paste, cardboard circle

- Display the letter cards *P* and *p*. As you point to each letter in turn, encourage volunteers to identify each as capital *P* or lowercase *p*. Say the word *pillow*. Explain that *pillow* begins with the letter *p*. Write the word *pillow*. Have a volunteer write over the letter *p*.
- Say the words *pickle* and *pillow*. Ask if the words begin with the same sound. Then read this sentence: *Peter Pan put a puzzle on a pirate ship*. Invite children to put their thumbs up for each word they hear that begins like *pillow*.
- Have children suggest other things Peter Pan could have put on the pirate ship that begins with the key sound. If they need help getting started, suggest *pizza, popsicle, peach,* or *parrot*. Repeat the tongue twister with the new words.

### Use the Page
- Write the number 42 on the chalkboard and say it aloud. Have children turn to page 42 in their books.
- Direct children's attention to the key picture and ask them to identify the letter that begins the word *pillow,* and then draw a line around the letter *p*.
- Point to the letter *p* on the lines in the pillow. Have children identify lowercase *p*. Invite them to write over the letter, starting at the red dot. You may wish to demonstrate the proper way to form the letter on the chalkboard. Then have children practice writing the letter *p*.
- Ask children to point to the picture of the pear. Have them say *pillow* and *pear*. Ask if the two words begin with the same letter and sound. Then point out the letter *p* above the pear, and have children write over the letter as they did in the key picture.
- Point out the remaining boxes and challenge children to identify the picture in each one. Explain that they will write *p* above each picture whose name begins with the same letter and sound as *pillow*.

- Cut out a large circle from cardboard and tell children to pretend it is a pizza. Distribute magazines, scissors, and paste. Ask children to cut out pictures of food items whose names begin with /p/*p* and paste them on their pizza. Some choices might include: pepperoni, pepper, peas, or unusual items such as pineapples and pears.
- Play "Cross the Pond" with the children. Mark an area on the floor to represent a pond. Ask the first child crossing the pond to say a word that begins with the letter *p*. If the response is correct, he or she crosses the pond. If the response is incorrect, he or she goes to the back of the line. Continue until everyone crosses the pond.
- Distribute drawing paper and crayons. Have children write *p* at the top of their paper. Then ask them to draw a picture of something whose name begins with /p/*p*.

**Final Consonant:** /p/*p*
Write these rhyming pairs on the chalkboard and read them together: *jeep/beep; top/stop; lip/sip*. Ask children how the words are alike. Brainstorm additional rhyming words ending with /p/*p*. Then write rhymes describing real things, people, or objects using the words on the list. Here are two examples:
*The jeep can beep.*
*The top will stop.*

**MEETING INDIVIDUAL NEEDS**

**Second-Language Support**
Non-native English speakers will benefit from demonstrating the action words used in the rhyming activity to internalize meaning.

# Auditory Discrimination: /l/*l*

DIRECTIONS: Help children identify the key picture at the top of the page. Then have them draw a line around the pictures that begin with the same sound as the word *lemon*. Have children think of other words that begin with the same sound as *lemon*.

Auditory Discrimination: /l/*l*    Children should also circle lion, lamb, log, leaves, lizard.

43

## OBJECTIVES

Phonics and Decoding Skills

Discriminate among initial sounds

Discriminate among final sounds

## MATERIALS

Real lemon or illustration of a lemon; chart paper; pictures or picture cards whose names begin with /l/*l* as well as other consonant sounds; picture cards for *seal, girl, quail, tiger, pencil,* and *key;* chart paper; **Sing a Sound Audiocassette**, Tape 2

## BUILD BACKGROUND

- Display a picture of a lemon (or a real lemon), and ask children to identify it. Invite children to pantomime eating a lemon. Ask why they wrinkle their noses or make other faces when eating a lemon. Elicit that a lemon is a small yellow fruit that is quite sour.
- Say the word *lemon*, emphasizing the beginning sound. Name other foods (including some whose names begin with /l/). Have children repeat only the words that begin with the same sound as *lemon: lettuce, lime, lollipop, licorice, lentils.*
- Read these word pairs. Ask children to clap their hands when both words in the pair begin with the same sound as *lemon: lion, love; big, little; leopard, lizard; listen, loud; leaf, tree; lamb, laugh; lap, leg.*

## DEVELOP/APPLY

### Use the Page

- Write the number 43 on the chalkboard and say it aloud. Have children turn to page 43 in their books.
- Direct children's attention to the key picture at the top of the page and have it identified. Have children identify the animals in the picture as well. Then invite them to look at the picture and tell what the lion and the lamb are doing.
- Point to the ladybug and have children identify it. Ask why the ladybug has a line drawn around it. (*Ladybug* begins with the same sound as *lemon.*) Have children say *lemon* and *ladybug* and then write over the line with a pencil.
- Encourage children to complete the page by drawing a line around each object whose name begins with the same sound as *lemon.* Ask children to say other words that begin like *lemon.*

## REINFORCE

- Take children on a "Listening and Looking Walk." Have them listen and look for things whose names begin with the same sound as *lemon.*
- Draw a ladder on chart paper. Place two picture cards on each rung of the ladder. Use pictures whose names begin with the same sound as *lemon,* as well as other consonant sounds. Have volunteers turn over each set of pictures and identify those whose names begin like *lemon,* as they climb the ladder.
- The song "Looby Loo" (**Sing a Sound Audiocassette**, Tape 2, Side 1) provides another way to reinforce /l/. After the children sing and dance along with the song, you might have half the class sing the song again, while the other half sings *la-la* after each line of the chorus.

## CHALLENGE

**Final Consonant:** /l/l
Display the picture card for *seal.* Have children name what it depicts. Emphasize the ending consonant sound. Have children repeat these words, listening for the ending /l/l: *pail, ball, doll, nail, camel.* Display the picture cards *girl, quail, tiger, pencil,* and *key.* Have children sort the pictures into two piles: words that end with the same sound as *seal* and words that do not.

---

**MEETING**
**INDIVIDUAL**
**NEEDS**

**Second-Language Support**
Pair non-native English speakers with native English speakers as they work on the /l/l activities. The sound /l/ is not used in the Spanish language and in some other languages. Children may benefit from hearing the sound produced by their partners.

# Initial Consonant: /l/ *l*

DIRECTIONS: Help children identify the letters and pictures. Ask them to draw a line around the letter *l* in the word *lemon* and write *l* on the lines. Then in each box, have children write the letter *l* above each picture that begins with the same letter and sound as the key picture.

lemon

1. ladder
2. egg
3. lamp
4. letter
5. leaf
6. lunchbox
7. lock
8. envelope

Macmillan/McGraw-Hill

44

Initial Consonant: /l/

## OBJECTIVES

Phonics and Decoding Skills

Recognize initial consonant: /l/ *l*

## MATERIALS

ABC cards or letter cards for *L* and *l*, picture cards or objects whose names begin with /l/ *l* and other consonants, yarn or shoelaces

- Display the letter cards *L* and *l*. As you point to each letter in turn, encourage volunteers to identify it as capital *L* or lowercase *l*. Say the word *lemon*. Explain that *lemon* begins with the letter *l*. Write the word *lemon*. Have a volunteer write over the letter *l*.
- Display picture cards along the chalkboard ledge. Have children select the pictures whose names begin with /l/l. Then, have children turn over the cards to check the letters, and trace over the letters *L* and *l* with their fingers.

## DEVELOP/APPLY

### Use the Page

- Write the number 44 on the chalkboard and say it aloud. Have children turn to page 44 in their books.
- Direct children's attention to the key picture and ask them to identify the letter that begins the word *lemon*. Then draw a line around the letter *l*.
- Point to the letter *l* on the lines in the lemon. Have children identify it as lowercase *l*. Invite them to write over the letter, starting at the red dot. You may wish to demonstrate the proper way to form the letter on the chalkboard. Then have children practice writing the letter *l*.
- Ask children to point to the picture of the ladder. Have them say *lemon* and *ladder*. Ask if the two words begin with the same letter and sound. Then point out the letter *l* above the ladder, and have children write over the letter as they did in the key picture.
- Point out the remaining boxes and challenge children to identify the picture in each one. Explain that they will write *l* above each picture whose name begins with the same letter and sound as *lemon*.

### Reading

Encourage children to study posters or signs displayed in the classroom and find words that begin with /l/l.

- Display pictures of objects whose names begin with *l*, including a lion and a lamp. Then read the riddles below. Challenge children to create their own riddles for words that begin with /l/l.

I have four legs and a tail.
I have a mane and I roar.
My name starts with the letter *l*.
What am I? *(lion)*

I have a cord and a plug.
I can make a room light up.
My name starts with the letter *l*.
What am I? *(lamp)*

- Display picture cards for *lamb, lion, lock, yo-yo,* and *vase*. Have children identify the three pictures whose names begin with /l/l. Ask children if they can make up a sentence for each picture name. Write the sentences on the chalkboard as volunteers dictate. Have children find and draw a line around the words that begin with *l*.
- Have children use laces (shoelaces, yarn laces) to form the letters *L* and *l*. Then ask them to create a picture of an object using the laces and crayons.

**Second-Language Support**
To help non-native English learners with riddles, you might have native speakers pantomime the clues after you say them. When the correct answer has been given, provide additional reinforcement by having all children repeat the answer.

# Auditory Discrimination: /o/o

DIRECTIONS: Help children identify the key picture at the top of the page. Then have them draw a line around the pictures that begin with the same sound as the word *olive*. Have children think of other words that begin with the same sound as *olive*.

Auditory Discrimination: /o/o    Children should also circle ostrich, otter, octopus.    45

## OBJECTIVES

Phonics and Decoding Skills

Discriminate among initial sounds

## MATERIALS

Picture of an olive or a real olive

## BUILD BACKGROUND

- Display a picture of an olive or show a real olive, and ask children to identify it. Invite children to tell where they have seen olives (perhaps on pizza, in salads, or in a vegetable dish). Explain that an olive is a small fruit that grows on a tree. It can be green or black.
- Say the word *olive* emphasizing the beginning sound. Then say the words *olive* and *octopus,* having children repeat the words after you. Ask children if the words begin with the same sound. Then say the word *apple* and ask if it begins with the same sound as *olive.*
- Have children pat their stomachs when they hear you say a word that begins with the same sound as *olive.* You may wish to use these words: *olive, otter; olive, October; olive, ant; olive, operator; olive, hog; olive, egg.*

## DEVELOP/APPLY

### Use the Page
- Write the number 45 on the chalkboard and say it aloud. Have children turn to page 45 in their books.
- Direct children's attention to the key picture at the top of the page and have it identified. Then have children identify the animals in the picture. Invite volunteers to tell what they know about each animal. Then ask children to tell a story that describes the action in the picture.
- Point to the ox and have children identify it. Ask why the ox has a line drawn around it. (*Ox* begins with the same sound as *olive.*) Have children say *olive* and *ox* and then write over the line with a pencil.
- Encourage children to complete the page by drawing a line around each object whose name begins with the same sound as *olive.* Ask children to name other words that begin like *olive.*

## REINFORCE

- Teach children the following chants, and then invite them to chant with you. Some children may enjoy tapping out the beat of the chant or creating a rap. Then have children raise their hands when they hear a word that begins with the same sound as *olive.*

  Otter, otter, splishing, splashing
  on the water.

  Ox, ox, get on the box!

- Have children march around the room as you slowly call out words. Tell them that when they hear a word that begins with the same sound as *olive,* they are to stop and salute. (Demonstrate a salute.)
- Teach the song "An Octopus" to reinforce the short *o* sound. After the children sing and dance along with the song, have them repeat each word that begins with the same sound as *olive.*

**An Octopus**
(Tune of "Did You Ever See a Lassie?")

An octopus has eight legs,
on his body, on his body.
An octopus has eight legs
to run the opposite way.

# Initial Vowel: /o/ *o*

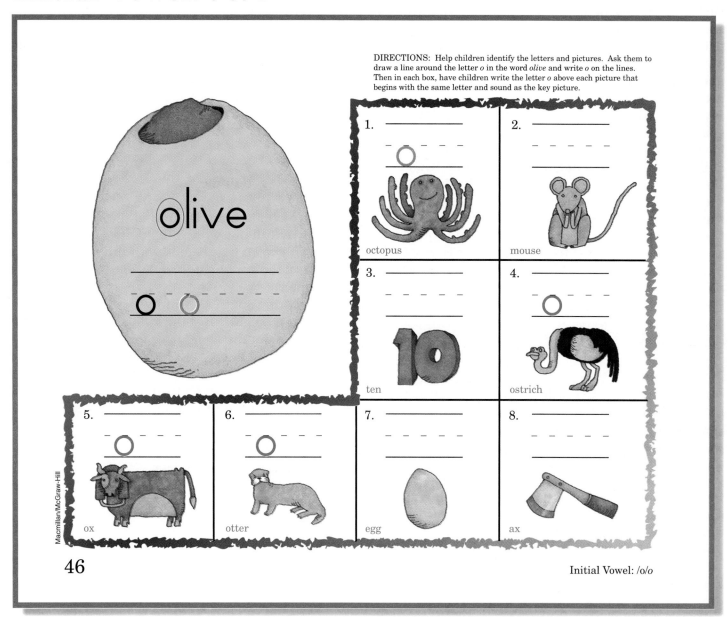

DIRECTIONS: Help children identify the letters and pictures. Ask them to draw a line around the letter *o* in the word *olive* and write *o* on the lines. Then in each box, have children write the letter *o* above each picture that begins with the same letter and sound as the key picture.

olive

o   o

1. octopus
2. mouse
3. ten
4. ostrich
5. ox
6. otter
7. egg
8. ax

Macmillan/McGraw-Hill

46

Initial Vowel: /o/*o*

## OBJECTIVES

Phonics and Decoding Skills

Recognize initial vowel: /o/*o*

Recognize medial vowel: /o/*o*

## MATERIALS

ABC cards or letter cards for *O* and *o*, picture cards or objects whose names begin with *o* and other letters, drawing paper, crayons, index cards

## BUILD BACKGROUND

- Display the letter cards *O* and *o*. As you point to each letter in turn, encourage volunteers to identify each as capital *O* or lowercase *o*. Say the word *olive*. Elicit from children that *olive* begins with the letter *o*. Write the word *olive*. Have a volunteer write over the letter *o*.
- Hold up picture cards, one at a time. Have children identify the pictures whose names begin with /o/o. Challenge them to think of other words that begin with the short *o* sound.

## DEVELOP/APPLY

### Use the Page
- Write the number 46 on the chalkboard and say it aloud. Have children turn to page 46 in their books.
- Direct children's attention to the key picture. Ask children to identify the letter that begins the word *olive* and then draw a line around the letter *o*.
- Point to the letter *o* on the lines in the olive. Have children identify lowercase *o*. Invite them to write over the letter, starting at the red dot. You may wish to demonstrate the proper way to form the letter on the chalkboard. Then have children practice writing the letter *o*.
- Ask children to point to the picture of the octopus. Have them say *olive* and *octopus*. Ask if the two words begin with the same letter and sound. Then point out the letter *o* above the octopus, and have children write over the letter as they did in the key picture.
- Point out the remaining boxes and challenge children to identify the picture in each one. Explain that they will write *o* above each picture whose name begins with the same letter and sound as the key picture.

### Writing
Make a class book in the shape of an olive. Invite children to draw pictures of words whose names begin with the same letter and sound as *olive*, or write the words.

## REINFORCE

- Give each child a sheet of drawing paper and crayons. Have children write *o*'s of different sizes and colors all over the paper. Then demonstrate for children how to turn an *o* into a funny face by adding eyes, a nose, a mouth, and hair. Encourage children to give their *o* faces different expressions. Display children's work.
- Write the words *otter* and *ostrich* on the chalkboard, and have children read them with you. Ask how the words are alike. Have children write each word on an index card, and then use it in a sentence.

## CHALLENGE

### Medial Vowel: /o/o
Ask children to listen for the /o/ in these two words: *olive* and *mop*. Help children understand that the short *o* sound is heard at the beginning of *olive* and in the middle of *mop*. Then say these words: *hot, mop, cob, rod, log, Mom*. Ask children to identify the sound they hear in the middle of each word. Remind children that /o/o can be heard at the beginning or in the middle of words. Children may want to record the words in their writing journals.

# Initial Consonants Review: /j/*j*, /m/*m*, /p/*p*, /l/*l*

DIRECTIONS: Review the letter forms with children. Then in each box, have children trace the letter and draw a line around the pictures with names that begin with that letter.

Initial Consonants Review: /j/*j*, /m/*m*, /p/*p*, /l/*l*

47

## OBJECTIVES

Phonics and Decoding Skills

Recognize initial consonants: /j/*j*, /m/*m*, /p/*p*, /l/*l*

Recognize final consonants: /m/*m*, /p/*p*, /l/*l*

## MATERIALS

ABC cards or letter cards for *Jj, Mm, Pp, Ll*; picture cards for *jet, mouse, pencil,* and *lion;* jar or bag; chart paper

- Display the letter cards for *J, j, M, m, P, p, L,* and *l.* Ask children to identify the letters as lowercase or capital.
- Display picture cards for *jet, mouse, pencil,* and *lion* and the letter cards *j, m, p,* and *l.* Ask children to name each object. Then ask children to name the letter that stands for the beginning sound in *jet.* Call on a volunteer to hold up the picture for *jet* and the letter card *j.* Continue in the same manner for each picture and initial letter and sound.

## DEVELOP/APPLY

### Use the Page
- Write the number 47 on the chalkboard and say it aloud. Have children turn to page 47 in their books.
- Direct children's attention to the first box on the left top of the page. Point to the letter and have children identify *j.* Tell children to write over the letter, starting at the red dot. You may wish to model how to form the letter on the chalkboard. Then point to the pictures in the box and have them identified. Ask children to name the pictures whose names begin with /j/*j,* and then draw a line around those pictures.
- In the box to the right, have children identify and write over the letter *m,* and then draw a line around the pictures whose names begin with /m/*m.*
- Continue this procedure with the letters *p* and *l.*

### Reading
Divide the class into four groups and assign one letter to each group. Have each group look for words posted around the school that begin with their assigned letter *j, m, p,* or *l.*

### Writing
Have each group record on chart paper the words they found posted around the school. Display each group's word list, and read the words with the children.

- Put the letter cards *J, j, M, m, P, p, L,* and *l* in a jar or bag. Call on a volunteer to pick a letter out of the jar and say a word that begins with that letter sound. Write each word on the chalkboard and read it aloud.
- Prepare children for a "Scavenger Hunt." Divide the class into four groups. Ask each group to find and collect two objects that begin with /j/*j,* two that begin with /m/*m,* two that begin with /p/*p,* and two that begin with /l/*l.* Allow a specific time limit for each hunt. At the end of the time, have each group share what they found.
- Distribute ABC cards for *j, m, p,* and *l,* and have children identify their letter. Then have a volunteer hold up his or her letter card and pantomime a word that begins with that letter. Invite the remaining children to guess the word.

## CHALLENGE

**Final Consonants**: /m/*m,* /p/*p,* /l/*l*
Display the letter cards *m, p,* and *l.* Hold up the letter card for *m,* say the word *mitten,* and have children tell whether they hear the /m/*m* sound at the beginning or at the end of the word. Continue this procedure using these words: *drum, tell, bull, gym, mattress, rope, tip, same, sell, pack, lunch.*

**Second-Language Support**
You might wish to pair native English speakers with non-native English speakers for the "Scavenger Hunt" to provide many opportunities to hear and say the key sounds in context.

# Listening, Speaking, Viewing

48

Listening, Speaking, Viewing

**OBJECTIVES**

Listening, Speaking, Viewing Skills

Apply Comprehension Strategies
in Viewing Activities

Identify categories

Identify picture details

Drawing conclusions

**MATERIALS**

*Zoo-Be-Doo* Big Book, white
construction paper, book rings,
magazines, glue, scissors, tape

## BUILD BACKGROUND

- Display the Big Book, *Zoo-Be-Doo*. Tell children that you will give them some clues about an animal or thing in the book. Begin by giving clues about a hippo. For example:
  *It lives near the water. It has a large body with short, chubby legs. It has a very large mouth.*
  When children guess the animal, turn to page 17 in the book and show them the animal. Invite them to add other information about the hippo. Continue by giving clues about a seal, iguana, vet, and keys.
- Read the book with the children. As you read, focus on punctuation. Together with children, point out periods, question marks, and exclamation points. Explain when each is used. You may wish to cover the punctuation mark at the end of some sentences and have children predict which mark is used and why.

## DEVELOP/APPLY

### Use the Page
- Write the number 48 on the chalkboard. Have children turn to page 48 in their books.
- Ask children what the boys and girls in the picture are making. You may want to explain that a scrapbook is a book in which you put pictures, newspaper articles, ribbons, postcards, notes, and other important items that you want to save.
- Help children discover what specific things the children in the picture are planning to put in their scrapbook: pictures of seals and iguanas; drawings of a rhinoceros; photographs of each other, the zookeeper, and the vet; postcards; and zoo posters. You should find that the items were all collected from their trip to the zoo.

### Reading
Explain that the children in the picture may want to sort the pictures and items before putting them in the scrapbook. They might want to start by dividing the animals into two groups with a page for big animals and a page for small animals. Ask children which animals would go on each page.

## REINFORCE

- Invite children to make a class scrapbook. (If you have been on a field trip recently, you may want to use that as the theme.) Look for photographs, pictures, postcards, and other items to put in the class scrapbook. Work together to write a title for the scrapbook and to label each item. Then help children arrange the items in the scrapbook. Display the scrapbook.
- Make a list of the items in the scrapbook created by the children on page 48: *seals, iguanas, rhinoceros, zookeeper, keys, vet*. Add to the list the items children placed in their own scrapbook. Read the words together.
- Draw a line under words that begin with the same letter, and ask children what these words have in common. Have them determine that each word begins with the same letter. Circle the initial letter in each word to emphasize the commonality. Have children categorize other words by their initial letters.
- Read other books about rhinoceroses, seals, and iguanas. You may wish to begin with these selections:

### Fiction
*How the Rhinoceros Got Its Skin* by Rudyard Kipling (Rabbit Ears, 1988).

*Sammy the Seal* by Syd Hoff (Harper and Row, 1959).

### Nonfiction
*Seal on the Rocks* by Doug Allan (G. Stevens, 1988).

*Iguanas* by L. Martin (Rourke, 1989).

*Seals* by Annette Barkhausen (G. Stevens, 1992).

# Letter Identification: *K, R, S, V, I*

DIRECTIONS: Have children point to each colored circle as you name it and then draw a line around the letter you name: yellow circle, *K*; red circle, *R*; blue circle, *S*; green circle, *V*; orange circle, *I*.

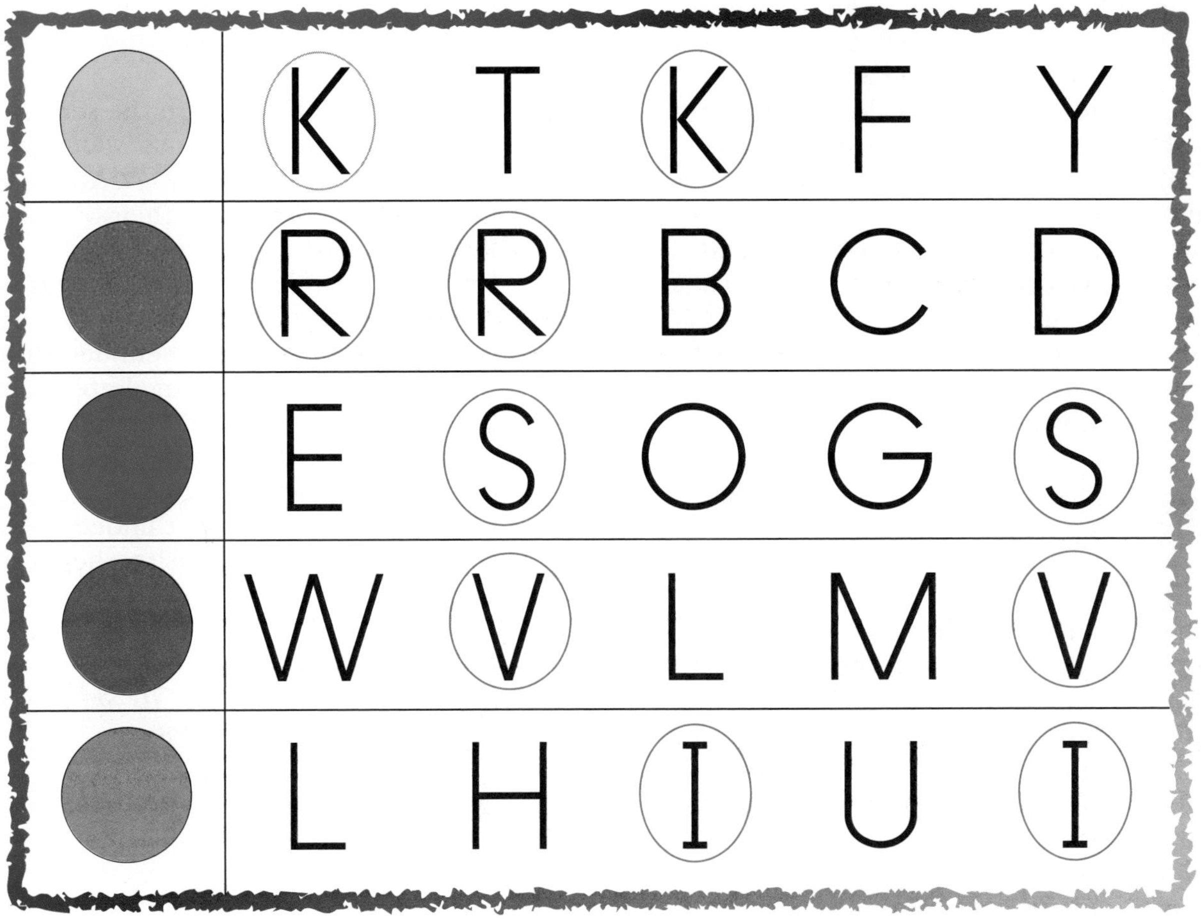

| | | | | | |
|---|---|---|---|---|---|
| ⬤ | K | T | Ⓚ | F | Y |
| ⬤ | Ⓡ | Ⓡ | B | C | D |
| ⬤ | E | Ⓢ | O | G | Ⓢ |
| ⬤ | W | Ⓥ | L | M | Ⓥ |
| ⬤ | L | H | Ⓘ | U | Ⓘ |

Letter Identification: *K, R, S, V, I*

49

## OBJECTIVES

Phonics and Decoding Skills

Identify capital letters: *K, R, S, V, I*

## MATERIALS

ABC cards or letter cards for *K, R, S, V, I*; alphabet chart; oaktag; marker; cassette or CD with music (optional); fingerpaint; fingerpaint paper

## ACTIVITIES
## BUILD BACKGROUND

- Display the letter cards for *K, R, S, V,* and *I* and an alphabet chart. Begin the lesson by having children match each letter, without naming it, to the same letter on the chart.
- Sing "The Alphabet Song" with the children. As you come to the letters *I, K, R, S,* and *V,* stop and point to that letter on the letter cards or on the alphabet chart.
- Have children point out the letters on name tags, posters, or other labels in the classroom.
- Distribute one letter card, *K, R, S, V,* or *I,* to each child. Write one of the letters on the chalkboard. Ask children who are holding the same letter card to stand and show their letters. Then have children say the name of the letter aloud before writing the letter on the chalkboard.

## DEVELOP/APPLY

**Use the Page**
- Write the number 49 on the chalkboard and say it aloud. Have children turn to page 49 in their books.
- Have children find and point to the yellow circle in the first row. Invite children to name the letters they know. Then ask a volunteer to name the letter in the first row that has a line around it. Have children draw a line around each capital *K* in the row.
- Next, ask children to point to the red circle in the second row, and name the letters they know. Then have them draw a line around each capital *R.*
- In the row with the blue circle, have children draw a line around each capital *S.*
- Continue in this way with the two remaining rows and capital letters *V* and *I.*

## ACTIVITIES
## REINFORCE

- Prepare five sets of letter cards for *K, R, S, V,* and *I* by writing each letter on a large oaktag square. Tape each letter square to the floor, forming a circle. Have children stand on the letters. Instruct them to move around the circle, from letter to letter, as music is played. When the music stops, ask all children to identify the letter they are standing on.
- Have children sit on the floor, one behind the other. Ask children to use their fingers to write a capital *K* on the back of the person sitting in front of them. You may wish to demonstrate this first. Repeat for capital *R, S, V,* and *I.*
- Provide fingerpaint and paper. Write the capital letters, *K, R, S, V,* and *I* on the chalkboard. Have children fingerpaint each capital letter on their paper.

# Letter Identification: *k, r, s, v, i*

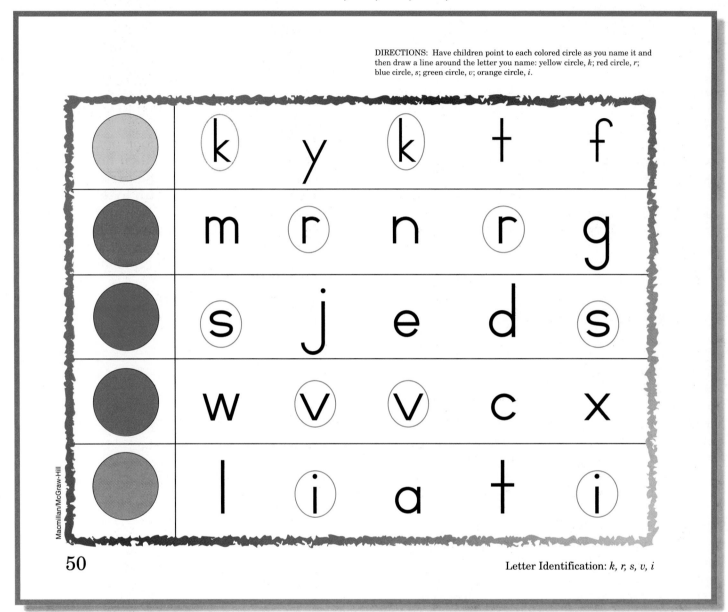

DIRECTIONS: Have children point to each colored circle as you name it and then draw a line around the letter you name: yellow circle, *k*; red circle, *r*; blue circle, *s*; green circle, *v*; orange circle, *i*.

Macmillan/McGraw-Hill

50

Letter Identification: *k, r, s, v, i*

## OBJECTIVES

Phonics and Decoding Skills

Identify lowercase letters: *k, r, s, v, i*

## MATERIALS

ABC cards or letter cards for *k, r, s, v, i*; alphabet chart; magazines; newspapers; paste; scissors; butcher paper; computer or typewriter

## BUILD BACKGROUND

- Distribute the letter cards *k, r, s, v,* and *i* to children. Write one of the letters on the chalkboard. Ask children who are holding the same letter card to stand, show their letter, and name their letter.
- As a follow-up to the activity above, have children with matching letters stand in a group together. Spark interest for letter formation by inviting children to use their bodies to create the letter. Switch letters and have the groups repeat the activity.
- Sing "The Alphabet Song" with the children. As you come to the letters *i, k, r, s,* and *v,* stop and point to that letter on the letter cards or on the alphabet chart. Then have children say the name of the letter aloud before writing it on the chalkboard.

## DEVELOP/APPLY

### Use the Page

- Write the number 50 on the chalkboard and say it aloud. Have children turn to page 50 in their books.
- Have children find and point to the yellow circle in the first row. Invite children to name the letters they know. Then ask a volunteer to name the letter in the first row that has a line around it. Have children draw a line around each lowercase *k* in the row.
- Next, ask children to point to the red circle in the second row, and name the letters they know. Then have them draw a line around each lowercase *r.*
- In the row with the blue circle, have children draw a line around each lowercase *s.*
- Continue in this way with the two remaining rows and lowercase letters *v* and *i.*

## REINFORCE

- Have each child find a partner. Ask one of the children in each pair to sit with their back to the chalkboard. Place the letter card for *k* on the chalkboard ledge. Have the children facing the chalkboard use their pointing finger to write the lowercase letter on their partner's hand. Encourage their partner to guess the letter. Have children change roles and continue.
- Invite children to practice typing the letters *k, r, s, v,* and *i* on a typewriter or a computer. Ask children to share their work in small groups, naming each letter as they point to it.
- Help children form small groups. Provide scissors, magazines, newspaper, paste, and a long sheet of butcher paper with one of the key letters printed on it: *k, r, s, v,* or *i.* Then ask children to find examples of their assigned letter, cut them out, and paste them on the butcher paper to make a mural.

# Auditory Discrimination: /k/*k*

DIRECTIONS: Help children identify the key picture at the top of the page. Then have them draw a line around the pictures that begin with the same sound as the word *kite*. Have children think of other words that begin with the same sound as *kite*.

Auditory Discrimination: /k/*k*   Children should also circle king, kangaroo, keys, kick.

51

## OBJECTIVES

Phonics and Decoding Skills

Discriminate among initial sounds

Discriminate among final sounds

## MATERIALS

Picture of a kite or a real kite, picture cards or objects whose names begin and end with /k/*k* and other consonant sounds, chart paper, **Sing a Sound Audiocassette**, Tape 2, letter cards for *k*

- Display a picture of a kite (or a real kite) and have it identified. Explain that a kite is a toy that is flown in the wind. Call on volunteers to share their personal experiences with kites (how they made a kite, how to fly a kite, adventures and mishaps they had flying kites, and unusual kites they have seen).
- Say the word *kite,* emphasizing the beginning sound. Then name other things whose names begin with the same sound as *kite,* and have children repeat the names: *kickball, koala, kitten, key.*
- Read the following pairs of words. Have children pull the string on an imaginary kite when both words in the pair begin with the same sound as *kite: key, kangaroo; ketchup, mustard; kind, Kim; kiss, kennel; Kevin, soccer; king, koala.*

## DEVELOP/APPLY

### Use the Page

- Write the number 51 on the chalkboard and say it aloud. Have children turn to page 51 in their books.
- Direct children's attention to the key picture at the top of the page and have it identified. Then help children identify the game being played by the animals on the page. Explain that soccer is a game where the ball is kicked into a goal. Invite children to use the picture clues to tell a story about the picture.
- Point to the kitten on the page. Ask why the kitten has a line drawn around it. (*Kitten* begins with the same sound as *kite.*) Have children say *kite* and *kitten* and then write over the line with a pencil.
- Encourage children to complete the page by drawing a line around each object whose name begins with the same sound as *kite.* Have children think of other things that begin with the same sound as *kite,* and list them on the chalkboard.

- Children may enjoy listening to the Australian song "Kookaburra" on **Sing a Sound Audiocassette,** Tape 2, Side 1. Provide children with the letter card *k.* Encourage them to hold up their letter cards whenever they hear /k/.
- Play "Over Your Head" with the children. Assign children into small groups. Distribute to each group a set of picture cards, face down, whose names begin with /k/*k*. Have one child select a picture card and hold it over his or her head, without looking at it. Have the other members of the group suggest clues to help the child guess what picture is on the card. Some suggestions follow:

  You can use it to unlock a door. (*key*)
  The wind makes it fly. (*kite*)
  It has a pouch to carry its baby. (*kangaroo*)

- Have children create sentences for each of these words: *king, kitten,* and *kangaroo.* Write their sentences on chart paper. Then have volunteers underline all the /k/*k* words.

**ACTIVITIES** **CHALLENGE**

**Final Consonant:** /k/*k, ck*
Say the words *tick, tock,* and *clock.* Have children say the words after you. Emphasize the ending consonant sound. Have children repeat these words after you, listening for the ending *k* sound: *Jack, block, Buck, talk.* Display the picture cards *sock, yak, seal, mask, door,* and *lock.* Let children sort the pictures into two piles: words that end like *clock* and words that do not.

**Auditory Discrimination: /k/*k* • 51a**

# Initial Consonant: /k/*k*

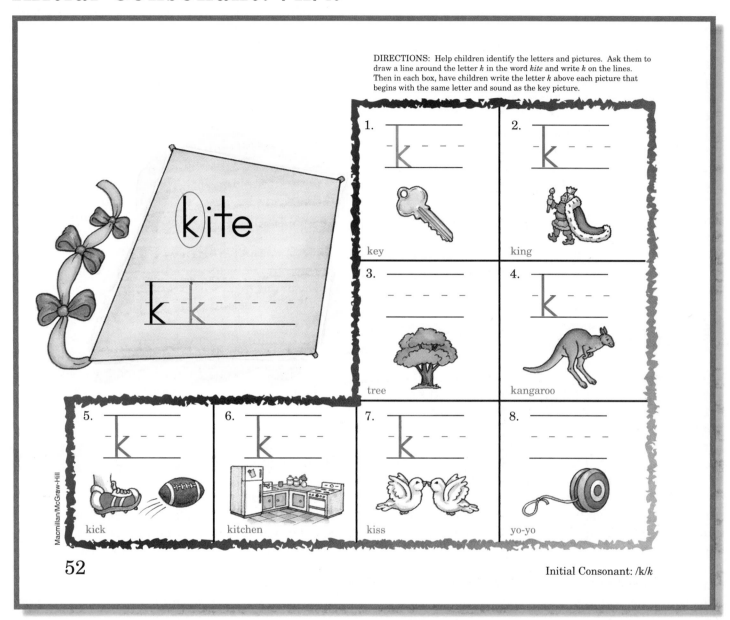

DIRECTIONS: Help children identify the letters and pictures. Ask them to draw a line around the letter *k* in the word *kite* and write *k* on the lines. Then in each box, have children write the letter *k* above each picture that begins with the same letter and sound as the key picture.

kite

k k

1. k — key
2. k — king
3. — tree
4. k — kangaroo
5. k — kick
6. k — kitchen
7. k — kiss
8. — yo-yo

Macmillan/McGraw-Hill

52

Initial Consonant: /k/*k*

## OBJECTIVES

Phonics and Decoding Skills

Recognize initial consonant: /k/*k*

Recognize final consonant: /k/*k*

## MATERIALS

ABC cards or letter cards for *K* and *k*, chart paper, wooden blocks, magnetic letters (optional)

- Display the letter cards *K* and *k*. As you point to each letter in turn, encourage volunteers to identify each as capital *K* or lowercase *k*. Say the word *kite*. Elicit from children that *kite* begins with the letter *k*. Write the word *kite*. Have a volunteer write over the letter *k*.
- Distribute a letter card for *K* or *k* to each child. Ask children to hold up their letter cards when they hear a word beginning with the same sound as *kite*. You may wish to use these words: *kiss, kick, jump, king, kitchen, bedroom, key, pillow, koala, Kevin.*
- Encourage volunteers to think of other /k/ words. Write these words on chart paper or, if possible, display the words using magnetic letters.

## DEVELOP/APPLY

### Use the Page
- Write the number 52 on the chalkboard and say it aloud. Have children turn to page 52 in their books.
- Direct children's attention to the key picture. Ask children to identify the letter at the beginning of the word *kite*, and then draw a line around the letter *k*.
- Point to the letter *k* on the lines in the kite. Have children identify lowercase *k*. Invite them to write over the letter, starting at the red dot. You may wish to demonstrate the proper way to form the letter on the chalkboard. Then have children practice writing the letter *k*.
- Ask children to point to the picture of the key. Have them say *kite* and *key*. Ask if the two words begin with the same letter and sound. Then point out the letter *k* above the key, and have children write over the letter as they did in the key picture.
- Point out the remaining boxes and challenge children to identify the picture in each one. Explain that they will write *k* above each picture whose name begins with the same letter and sound as *kite*.

- Have children lay wooden blocks on the floor to form the letter *k*. Encourage creativity by having children build structures whose names begin with /k/*k*, such as a *kitchen, kennel,* or *kingdom.*
- Play "Duck, Duck, Koala." Have children sit in a circle on the floor. Place a letter card for the letter *k* in the center of the circle and have children identify the letter name and some words that begin with the same sound as *kite*. To play the game, walk around the circle lightly touching each child on the shoulder as you name an object. When you touch a child and say an object whose name begins with /k/*k*, the child stands and chases you around the circle until you reach his or her spot. If the child touches you, he or she becomes "It," and must follow the same procedure until the next person is caught.
- Teach "Found a Key Ring" to the children. Ask children to think about what they might see when they open a mysterious door with the key. Invite children to substitute their own *k* words in the song to tell what they might discover.

> **Found a Key Ring**
> (Tune of "Found a Peanut")
>
> Found a key ring, found a key ring,
> found a key ring just now.
> Just now I found a key ring,
> found a key ring just now.

## CHALLENGE

**Final Consonant:** /k/*k*
Pantomime kicking a football. Ask children to suggest a word that describes the action (*kick*). Say it several times, having children repeat it after you. Explain that the word *kick* begins and ends with the sound of *k*. Say these words and have volunteers identify where they hear the *k* sound in each: *karate, rock, kindergarten, kit, truck, stack, kayak.*

# Auditory Discrimination: /r/r

DIRECTIONS: Help children identify the key picture at the top of the page. Then have them draw a line around the pictures that begin with the same sound as the word *rocket*. Have children think of other words that begin with the same sound as *rocket*.

Auditory Discrimination: /r/r     Children should also circle robot, rhinoceros, radio.     53

## OBJECTIVES

Phonics and Decoding Skills

Discriminate among initial sounds

Discriminate among final sounds

## MATERIALS

Picture or illustration of a rocket, objects or pictures of objects whose names begin with /r/r, basket, drawing paper, crayons, **Sing a Sound Audiocassette**, Tape 3

## BUILD BACKGROUND

- Show a picture or an illustration of a rocket. Have children identify the object and tell what they know about it. Explain that a rocket is a vehicle that travels through space.
- Say the words *rocket* and *rose* aloud. Ask if the words begin with the same sound. Then say the word *moon* and ask if it begins like *rocket*.
- Ask children to pretend their pointer finger is a rocket. Say the following word pairs and have children "launch their rockets" if both words in the pair begin with the same sound as rocket: *rail, ruler; roar, ribbon; red, blue; rooster, rug; radio, television; radish, ripe.*

## DEVELOP/APPLY

### Use the Page
- Write the number 53 on the chalkboard and say it aloud. Have children turn to page 53 in their books.
- Direct children's attention to the key picture at the top of the page and have it identified. Then invite children to describe the scene by telling a story about the animals' space adventure. You may wish to prompt children with these questions: *Who are the astronauts? What is the rhinoceros doing? What is the rabbit doing?*
- Then point to the rabbit in the picture. Encourage children to tell why a line has been drawn around the rabbit. (*Rabbit* begins with the same sound as *rocket.*) Have children say the words *rabbit* and *rocket,* and then trace over the line around the rabbit.
- Have children complete the page by drawing a line around each object whose name begins with the same sound as *rocket.* Ask children to think of other words that begin with the same sound as *rocket.*

## REINFORCE

- Write the title "Little Red Riding Hood" on the chalkboard. Read the title and ask children to point out the words that begin with /r/r.
- Place a basket on the floor and tell children to pretend that it belongs to Little Red Riding Hood. Have children collect classroom objects or draw pictures of objects beginning with /r/r. Place the objects and pictures in the basket.
- Play a game based on the plot of "Little Red Riding Hood." Assign children the parts of Grandmother, the wolf, and Little Red Riding Hood. Give Little Red Riding Hood the basket from the previous activity. Instruct her to pretend to pick flowers to bring to Grandmother. When the wolf enters, Little Red Riding Hood escapes by holding up an object or picture from the basket and using its name in a sentence. Little Red Riding Hood runs to Grandmother's house, and then gives Grandmother something from her basket beginning with /r/r. This time Grandmother uses that word in a sentence. Continue until all children have had an opportunity to play one of the characters.
- For added reinforcement of the sound /r/, you may wish to play the song "When the Red, Red Robin Comes Bob, Bob, Bobbin' Along" on **Sing a Sound Audiocassette,** Tape 3, Side 1. Have children bob up and down whenever they hear the words *red, red robin.*

## CHALLENGE

**Final Consonant:** /r/r
Say the following words and have children repeat each one after you: *car, jar, feather, bear, door.* Ask how the words are alike. Help children recognize that all the words end with /r/r. Challenge children to think of words rhyming with *car.* Point out that all of the rhyming words end with the sound. Then use the rhyming words to make a two-line rhyme or poem.

# Initial Consonant: /r/r

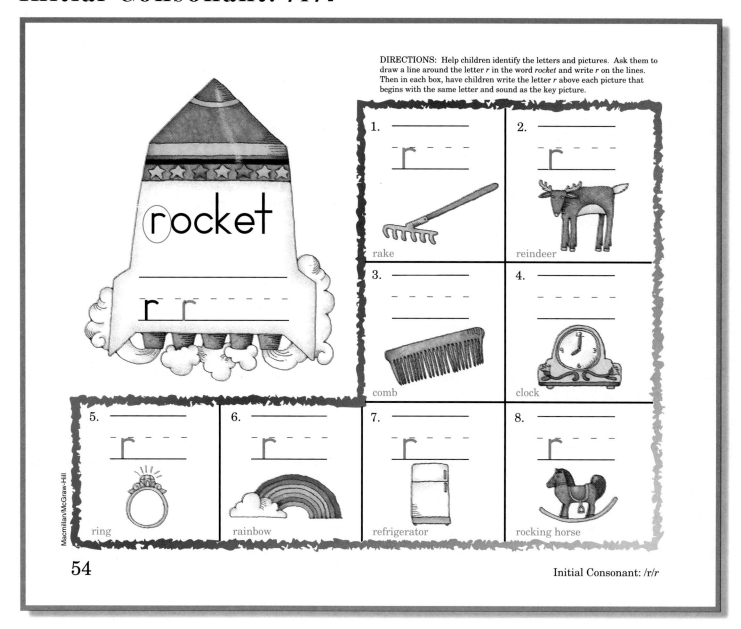

DIRECTIONS: Help children identify the letters and pictures. Ask them to draw a line around the letter *r* in the word *rocket* and write *r* on the lines. Then in each box, have children write the letter *r* above each picture that begins with the same letter and sound as the key picture.

rocket

r  r

1. _____ rake

2. _____ reindeer

3. _____ comb

4. _____ clock

5. _____ ring

6. _____ rainbow

7. _____ refrigerator

8. _____ rocking horse

Macmillan/McGraw-Hill

54

Initial Consonant: /r/r

## OBJECTIVES

Phonics and Decoding Skills

Recognize initial consonant: /r/r

Recognize final consonant: /r/r

## MATERIALS

ABC cards or letter cards for *R* and *r*, picture cards, chalk or masking tape, cardboard shapes, ribbon, cardboard box, hangers, string, crayons, magazines, scissors, newspapers

## BUILD BACKGROUND

- Display the letter cards *R* and *r*. As you point to each letter in turn, encourage volunteers to identify each as a capital *R* or lowercase *r*. Say the word *rocket*. Explain that *rocket* begins with the letter *r*. Write the word *rocket* on the chalkboard. Have a volunteer write over the letter *r*.
- Ask children which of these words begins with the same sound as *rocket*: *ring* or *watch*. Read the sentence that follows: *Little Red Riding Hood reads rhymes and riddles.* Invite children to draw a ring in the air for each word they hear that begins with the same sound as *ring* and *rocket*.
- Have children suggest other things that Little Red Riding Hood might do beginning with /r/*r*, such as: *ride a rollercoaster, run a race, rope a reindeer,* or *reach for a ripe, red radish.* Repeat the tongue twister with the new words.

## DEVELOP/APPLY

### Use the Page
- Write the number 54 on the chalkboard and say it aloud. Have children turn to page 54 in their books.
- Direct children's attention to the key picture, and have it identified as a rocket. Ask children to name the letter at the beginning of *rocket*, and then draw a line around the letter *r*.
- Point to the letter *r* on the lines in the rocket. Have children identify lowercase *r*. Invite them to write over the letter, starting at the red dot.
- Ask children to point to the picture of the rake. Have them say *rocket* and *rake*. Ask if the two words begin with the same letter and sound. Then point out the letter *r* above the rake and have children write over the letter.
- Point out the remaining boxes and challenge children to identify the picture in each one. Explain that they will write *r* above each picture whose name begins with the same letter and sound as *rocket*.

## REINFORCE

- Display a large box to represent a refrigerator. Set out magazines, picture cards, and newspapers. Have groups of children cut out pictures of food items whose names begin with /r/*r* and put them in the refrigerator. Some possible foods might include: *raisins, roast, rye, radishes, rutabaga, root beer, ravioli, rolls,* and *rice.*
- Make *r* mobiles. Distribute several cardboard shapes to each child. Instruct children to write the letter *r* on half of the shapes. Have them draw pictures of objects whose names begin with the /r/ sound on the other shapes. Punch a hole in the top and bottom of each shape and string several shapes together with lengths of ribbon. Hang each string of shapes from a plastic hanger.

## CHALLENGE

**Final Consonant:** /r/*r*
Say the word *roar* emphasizing both the beginning and ending consonant sounds. Ask children where they hear the /r/*r* sound. Elicit that the word begins and ends with the same sound and letter. Then write these words on the chalkboard: *car, oar, star, four, stir, chair, bear.* Have children say the words and then draw a line under the final *r*.

### MEETING INDIVIDUAL NEEDS

**Second-Language Support**
Encourage non-native English speakers to add pictures of foods common in their cultures to the "refrigerator." Invite them to tell other children about the food. As a follow-up, you may wish to prepare the food to let the class sample it. Some examples might include: rice cakes, rotis, refried beans, rigatoni, and roe.

# Auditory Discrimination: /s/s

DIRECTIONS: Help children identify the key picture at the top of the page. Then have them draw a line around the pictures that begin with the same sound as the word *sun*. Have children think of other words that begin with the same sound as *sun*.

Auditory Discrimination: /s/s

Children should also circle sunglasses, sand dollar, soap, sandals, submarine, sea horse, sailboat, seagull, sandpiper.

55

## OBJECTIVES

Phonics and Decoding Skills

Discrimination among initial sounds

Recognize final consonant: /s/s

## MATERIALS

Picture or illustration of the sun, suitcase or bag, **Sing a Sound Audiocassette**, Tape 3

## BUILD BACKGROUND

- Show a picture of the sun and have it identified. Invite children to share what they know about the sun. Explain that the sun provides light and heat for the Earth.
- Say the words *sun* and *soup* aloud. Ask if the words begin with the same sound. Then say the word *web* and ask if it begins like *sun*.
- Say the following word pairs. Have children make a sun with their arms if both words in the pair begin with the same sound as *sun*: *sun, parrot; sun, sing; sun, girl; sun, sew; sun, bark; sun, sandwich; sun, rock; sun, silly.*

## DEVELOP/APPLY

### Use the Page

- Write the number 55 on the chalkboard and say it aloud. Have children turn to page 55 in their books.
- Point to the key picture at the top of the page and have children identify it as the sun. Invite children to describe the action in the scene by telling a story about the girl's day at the beach. You may wish to prompt children with these questions: *Who is in the water? What are they doing? Who is on the shore? What is the girl wearing to protect her eyes?* Encourage children to identify the different things they see in the picture.
- Then point to the seal in the picture. Encourage children to tell why a line has been drawn around the seal. Explain that the word *seal* begins with the same sound as *sun*. Have children say the words *seal* and *sun*, and then trace over the line around the seal.
- Have children complete the page by drawing a line around each object whose name begins with the same sound as *sun*. Ask children to think of other words that begin with the same sound as *sun*.

## REINFORCE

- Remind children of the things they saw on page 55 (seal, sea horse, submarine, soap, sunglasses). Have volunteers create a sentence using each *s* word.
- Place a suitcase (or a bag) on the floor and tell children that you are going on a trip. Ask children to help you pack the suitcase by saying words that begin with the same sound as *sun*, such as *sock* and *sandwich*. Ask volunteers to walk to the suitcase and pretend to pack the object if its name begins like *sun*.
- Have children clap their hands twice when they hear a word beginning with the same sound as *sun*. Use these words: *soup, ran, dish, seat, sip, queen, sad, sour, many.*
- Tell children that you will make up a sentence that is missing a word. Explain that the word begins with the same sound as *sun*. Call on volunteers to identify the missing words. Use these sentences:
  1. I wear *(socks)* on my feet.
  2. This is a tuna *(sandwich)*.
  3. The *(seal)* slept in the zoo.
  4. The *(sun)* shines brightly in the sky.
  5. Mom made some hot vegetable *(soup)*.

- As an additional activity for the sound /s/, you may wish to play the song "Sing" by Joe Raposo (**Sing a Sound Audiocassette**, Tape 3, Side 1). Encourage children to clap their hands whenever they hear a word that begins with the same sound as *sun*.

## CHALLENGE

### Final Consonant: /s/s

Have children repeat these words after you, listening for the /s/ at the end of each word: *bus, gas, miss, kiss, Jess, pass.* Invite children to think of other words that end with the same sound.

## Initial Consonant: /s/s

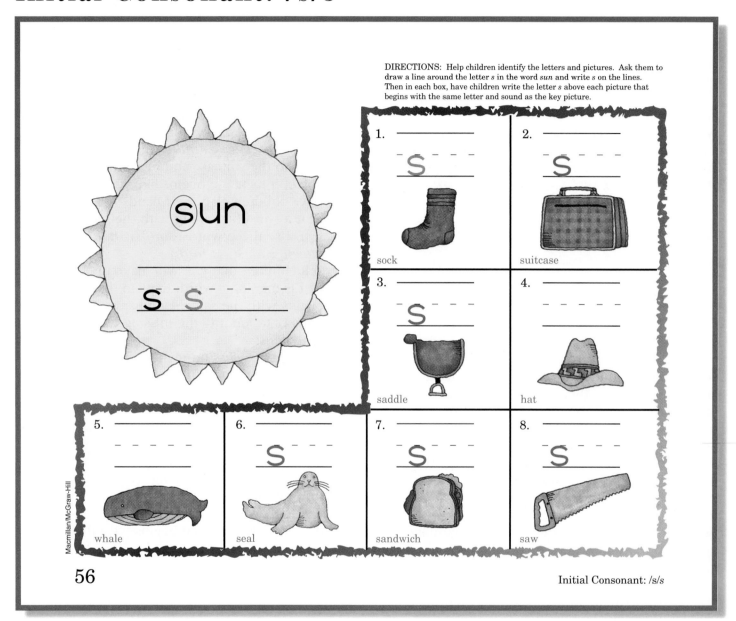

DIRECTIONS: Help children identify the letters and pictures. Ask them to draw a line around the letter *s* in the word *sun* and write *s* on the lines. Then in each box, have children write the letter *s* above each picture that begins with the same letter and sound as the key picture.

sun

s s

1. sock

2. suitcase

3. saddle

4. hat

5. whale

6. seal

7. sandwich

8. saw

Macmillan/McGraw-Hill

56

Initial Consonant: /s/s

## OBJECTIVES

Phonics and Decoding Skills

Recognize initial consonant: /s/s

Recognize final consonant: /s/s

## MATERIALS

ABC cards or letter cards for *S* and *s*, sandbox

- Display the letter cards *S* and *s*. As you point to each letter in turn, encourage volunteers to identify each as capital *S* or lowercase *s*. Say the word *sun*. Elicit from children that *sun* begins with the letter *s*. Write the word *sun* on the chalkboard, and have a volunteer write over the letter *s*.
- Distribute letter cards for *s* to the children. Have them hold up the letter cards when they hear words that begin with the same sound as *sun*. You may wish to use these words: *sandwich, salt, key, sausage, Sandy, paint, salad, joke, summer, October, September.*

## DEVELOP/APPLY

### Use the Page
- Write the number 56 on the chalkboard and say it aloud. Have children turn to page 56 in their books.
- Direct children's attention to the key picture. Ask children to name the letter at the beginning of *sun,* and then draw a line around the letter *s*.
- Point to the letter *s* on the lines in the sun. Have children identify lowercase *s*. Invite them to write over the letter, starting at the red dot. You may wish to demonstrate the proper way to form the letter on the chalkboard. Then have children practice writing the letter *s*.
- Ask children to point to the picture of the sock. Have them say *sun* and *sock*. Ask if the two words begin with the same letter and sound. Then point out the letter *s* above the sock and have children write over the letter.
- Point out the remaining boxes and challenge children to identify the picture in each one. Explain that they will write *s* above each picture whose name begins with the same letter and sound as *sun*.

### Reading
Have children study posters in the school to find words beginning with *s*.

- Have children write the letter *s* in the sand at a sand table or in the sandbox. Ask them to draw pictures of different *s* words in the sand, as well.
- Write the following fingerplay on the chalkboard and read it with the children. Then recite the words as you add appropriate hand motions to pantomime the actions: *work* (pull hoe), *plant* (drop seeds), *rain* (flutter fingers down), *sunshine* (make circle with hands), *grow* (flutter fingers up). Call on volunteers to underline the words that begin with the same letter and sound as *sun*.

**Seeds**

I work in my garden,
Plant seeds in a row;
The rain and the sunshine
Will help the seeds grow.

- Tell children that you will name some plants that could grow in a garden. Have them pretend to grow plants by fluttering their fingers up when a word that begins with the same sound as *sun* is read: *sunflower, tulip, seedling, rose, soapweed, daisy*. List the *s* words on the chalkboard as children name them, pointing to the beginning letter.

**Final Consonant:** /s/s
Ask children to listen for the /s/s sound as you say these words: *kiss, sad*. Challenge them to discover that one word begins with /s/s and one word ends with /s/s. Then say these words: *bus, sub, gas,* and *sag*. Repeat each word and ask children where they hear the *s* sound.

# Auditory Discrimination: /v/v

DIRECTIONS: Help children identify the key picture at the top of the page. Then have them draw a line around the pictures that begin with the same sound as the word *van*. Have children think of other words that begin with the same sound as *van*.

Auditory Discrimination: /v/v    Children should also circle vet, vase, vegetables, vacuum cleaner, vest.    57

## OBJECTIVES

Phonics and Decoding Skills

Discrimination among initial sounds

## MATERIALS

Picture or illustration of a van, ball of green yarn, **Sing a Sound Audiocassette**, Tape 3

## BUILD BACKGROUND

- Display a picture of a van and ask children to identify it. Invite children who have ridden in a van to tell how it is different from a car. Explain that a van is a type of vehicle for moving people or materials from place to place.
- Say the words *van* and *vase* aloud. Ask if the words begin with the same sound. Then say the word *book* and ask if it begins like *van*.
- Show children how to make the letter *v* with their index and middle fingers. Tell them to make a *v* when they hear you say a word that begins with the same sound as *van*. Use these words: *vinegar, baby, vacation, vacuum, vent, basket, visit, camp, map, vine.*

## DEVELOP/APPLY

### Use the Page

- Write the number 57 on the chalkboard and say it aloud. Have children turn to page 57 in their books.
- Point to the key picture at the top of the page and have children identify it as a van. Invite children to look at the big picture and pretend to be a puppy; then ask them to tell a story about going to the veterinarian's office.
- Point to the violets in the picture. Encourage children to tell why a line has been drawn around them. (*Violets* begins with the same sound as *van*.) Have children say the words *violets* and *van* and then trace over the line using their pencils.
- Encourage children to complete the page by drawing a line around each object whose name begins with the same sound as *van*. Have children think of other words that begin with the same sound as *van*.

## REINFORCE

- Instruct children to listen to the rhymes that follow. Have them complete each rhyme by suggesting a word that begins with the same sound as *van*.

I got dressed to look my best
And put on my brand new *(vest).*

I must feed and take my pet
to get his shots at the *(vet).*

- Have children make a vine by sitting in a circle on the floor. Hold one end of the yarn and roll the ball of yarn to a child. The child who receives the ball of yarn must say a word beginning with the same sound as *vine*. Then the child holds onto the yarn and rolls the ball to another child. The second player names a different word beginning with the same sound as *vine* before rolling the ball to someone else. Play continues, in this way, until several children have had a turn to name a /v/v word and become part of the yarn vine that winds around the circle.
- As an additional activity for the sound /v/, you may wish to play the song "Vadee, Veedee, Videe, Vodee, Voo" (**Sing a Sound Audiocassette**, Tape 3, Side 2). Encourage children to add another stanza.

### Second-Language Support

Expand knowledge and vocabulary associated with the key picture *van*. Pair non-native English speakers with native English speakers to look for vans as they pass the school or park at the school. Have the children decide whether the vans are used to move people or materials like food or building and plumbing materials.

# Initial Consonant: /v/*v*

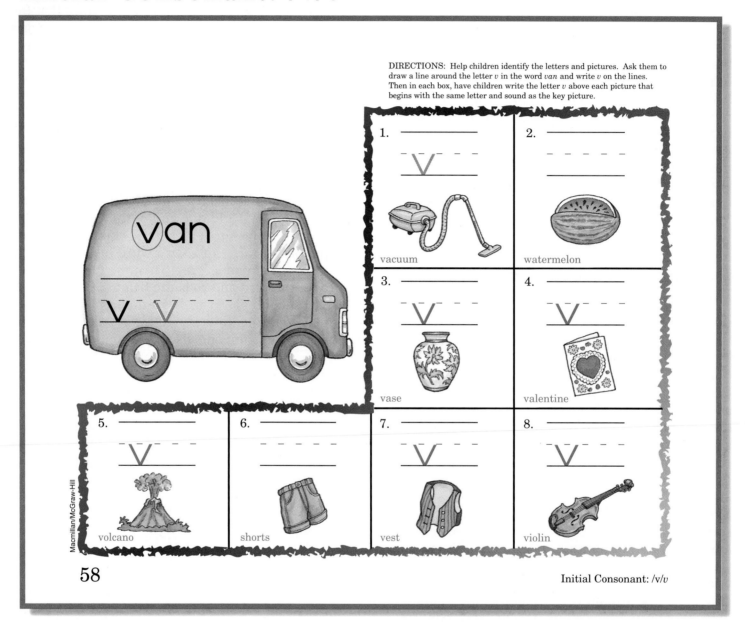

DIRECTIONS: Help children identify the letters and pictures. Ask them to draw a line around the letter *v* in the word *van* and write *v* on the lines. Then in each box, have children write the letter *v* above each picture that begins with the same letter and sound as the key picture.

1. _____ vacuum

2. _____ watermelon

3. _____ vase

4. _____ valentine

5. _____ volcano

6. _____ shorts

7. _____ vest

8. _____ violin

Macmillan/McGraw-Hill

58

Initial Consonant: /v/*v*

## OBJECTIVES

Phonics and Decoding Skills

Recognize initial consonant: /v/*v*

## MATERIALS

ABC cards or letter cards for *V* and *v*, picture cards for objects whose names begin with *v*, drawing paper, bag

## BUILD BACKGROUND

- Display the letter cards *V* and *v*. As you point to each letter in turn, encourage volunteers to identify them as capital *V* or lowercase *v*. Say the word *van*. Elicit from children that *van* begins with the letter *v*. Write the word *van* on the chalkboard. Have a volunteer write over the letter *v* as you identify it.
- Distribute letter cards for *v* to the children. Have them hold up the letter cards when they hear you say a word that begins with the same sound as *van*. You may wish to use these words: *valentine, visit, people, volunteer, video, candle, balloon, vitamin, volcano, pudding, voice, violin.*

## DEVELOP/APPLY

### Use the Page
- Write the number 58 on the chalkboard and say it aloud. Have children turn to page 58 in their books.
- Direct children's attention to the key picture. Ask children to name the letter at the beginning of *van,* and then draw a line around the letter *v*.
- Point to the letter *v* on the lines in the van. Have children identify lowercase *v*. Invite them to write over the letter, starting at the red dot. You may wish to demonstrate the proper way to form the letter on the chalkboard. Then have children practice writing the letter *v*.
- Ask children to point to the picture of the vacuum. Have them say *van* and *vacuum*. Ask if the two words begin with the same letter and sound. Point out the letter *v* above the vacuum; have children write over the letter.
- Point out the remaining boxes. Challenge children to identify each picture. Explain that they will write *v* above each picture whose name begins with the same letter and sound as *van*.

### Writing
Have children choose their favorite *v* word and use it in a sentence. Have them write the sentence in their Journals.

## REINFORCE

- Place pictures of objects whose names begin with /v/*v* in a bag. Invite volunteers, in turn, to pick a picture from the bag and give clues about the object. Have the other children guess the name of the object.
- Distribute drawing paper. Show children how to fold the paper in half vertically. Have them practice writing *V* on one side of the paper and *v* on the other. Display children's work.
- Brainstorm with children a list of objects whose names begin with the same sound as *van*. Write the words on the chalkboard. Then, write this sentence on the chalkboard:

*I'm going on vacation and I'm taking a _____.*

Ask children to complete the sentence with one of the words they named beginning with /v/*v*.

### Second-Language Support
The /v/*v* does not appear in Spanish; /v/ in Spanish is generally pronounced /b/. You may wish to place non-native English speakers in small groups with native English speakers so they may hear the sounds pronounced correctly.

# Auditory Discrimination: /i/ *i*

DIRECTIONS: Help children identify the key picture at the top of the page. Then have them draw a line around the pictures that begin with the same sound as the word *ink*. Have children think of other words that begin with the same sound as *ink*.

Auditory Discrimination: /i/*i*     Children should also circle insects, invitation.

59

## OBJECTIVES

Phonics and Decoding Skills

Discrimination among initial sounds

## MATERIALS

Picture or illustration of a bottle of ink, ink-filled pen, picture cards for *inner tube, insects, igloo, turkey, rabbit*

- Display a picture of a bottle of ink (or hold up a real bottle) and ask children to identify it. Explain that some writing pens are filled with ink. If possible, display an ink-filled pen.
- Say the words *ink* and *itch*, and have children repeat the words after you. Ask children if the words begin with the same sound. Then say the word *acorn* and ask if it begins with the same sound as *ink*.
- Have children scratch an itch when they hear you say a word that begins with the same sound as *ink* and *itch*. You may wish to use these words: *insect, in, out, instrument, imagine, button,* and *inside.*

### DEVELOP/APPLY

**Use the Page**

- Write the number 59 on the chalkboard and say it aloud. Have children turn to page 59 in their books.
- Identify the key picture on the top of the page as *ink*. Then have children identify the people in the scene. Encourage volunteers to tell what they know about very cold regions of the world. Then invite children to tell a story that describes the action in the picture. You may wish to prompt children with these questions: *What kind of house do the people here live in? What is the Eskimo doing? Why? Where do you see fish? Where do you think the fish came from?*
- Now point to the igloo in the picture. Ask children why it has a line drawn around it. (*Igloo* begins with the same sound as *ink*.) Have children say *ink* and *igloo,* and then trace over the line around the igloo.
- Encourage children to complete the page by drawing a line around each object whose name begins with the same sound as *ink*. Have children think of other words that begin with the same sound as *ink*.

- Play "Igloo Invitation" with the children. Have one child sit under a table and play the role of an Eskimo in an igloo. Other children walk around the icy igloo. Explain that they can get out of the cold and join the Eskimo inside the warm igloo by whispering a word that begins with the same sound as *ink*. Choose a new Eskimo and begin the game again when the "igloo" becomes too crowded.
- Say the following words and have children suggest a rhyming word that begins with the same sound as *ink*:

*fin, win (in)*
*witch, ditch (itch)*
*sink, pink (ink)*
*pinch, finch (inch)*
*bill, hill (ill)*
*sit, fit (it)*

- As an additional activity for the /i/ sound, sing the song "Inchworm" with the children. Have them draw a picture of an inchworm and label their picture.

**Inchworm**

Inchworm, inchworm following arithmetic.
You and your arithmetic will probably go far.
Two and two are four.
Four and four are eight.
Eight and eight are sixteen.
Sixteen and sixteen are thirty-two.

- Display the picture cards for *igloo, insects, turkey, rabbit,* and *inner tube* on the chalkboard ledge and have them identified. Have volunteers say the name of each picture again, listening for the beginning sound. Have them turn over the pictures whose names do not begin with the same sound as *ink*.

**Auditory Discrimination**: /i/*i* • **59a**

# Initial Vowel: /i/ *i*

DIRECTIONS: Help children identify the letters and pictures. Ask them to draw a line around the letter *i* in the word *ink* and write *i* on the lines. Then in each box, have children write the letter *i* above each picture that begins with the same letter and sound as the key picture.

1. igloo

2. easel

3. itch

4. invitation

5. insects

6. worm

7. fish

8. bow

Macmillan/McGraw-Hill

60

Initial Vowel: /i/*i*

## OBJECTIVES

Phonics and Decoding Skills

Recognize initial vowel: /i/ *i*

Spell words with vowel: /i/ *i*

## MATERIALS

ABC cards or letter cards for *I* and *i*, clay, fingerpaint paper and fingerpaint

- Display the letter cards *I* and *i*. As you point to each letter in turn, encourage volunteers to identify each as capital *I* or lowercase *i*. Say the word *ink*. Explain that *ink* begins with the letter *i*. Write the word *ink*. Have a volunteer write over the letter *i* as you identify it.
- Distribute letter cards for *i* to the children. Have them hold up the letter card when they hear you say a word that begins with the same sound as *ink*. You may wish to use these words: *inside, outside, inner tube, instant, acorn, it, incomplete, iguana, each, instrument, invite, party.*

## DEVELOP/APPLY

### Use the Page
- Write the number 60 on the chalkboard and say it aloud. Have children turn to page 60 in their books.
- Direct children's attention to the key picture. Ask children to identify the letter at the beginning of the word *ink* and then draw a line around the letter *i*.
- Point to the letter *i* on the lines in the ink bottle. Have children identify the lowercase *i*. Invite them to write over the letter, starting at the red dot. You may wish to demonstrate the proper way to form the letter on the chalkboard. Then have children practice writing the letter *i*.
- Ask children to point to the picture of the igloo. Have them say *ink* and *igloo*. Ask if the two words begin with the same letter and sound. Then point out the letter *i* above the *igloo*, and have children write over the letter.
- Point out the remaining boxes and ask children to identify the picture in each one. Explain that they will write *i* above each picture whose name begins with the same letter and sound as *ink*.

### Reading
Have children look at their favorite picture books to find words beginning with /i/*i*.

- Play the "Instant Group Game" with the children. Tell children that you are going to say four words. Explain that three of the words belong together in the same group. Children should name the three words belonging together and explain why. Then they think of a word beginning with /i/*i* to name the group.

  butterfly, ant, beetle, grass
  *(Group: Insects)*

  trumpet, rake, piano, drum
  *(Group: Instruments)*

- Invite children to use clay to mold crawly insects and other animals. Be sure to make a card to identify each animal. Use these clues to get children thinking about *i* animals.

  Clue 1: Bumblebees, grasshoppers, and ladybugs are this type of animal. *(insect)*
  Clue 2: This animal is a kind of large, green lizard. *(iguana)*
  Clue 3: This worm moves about an inch with every step it takes. *(inchworm)*

- Distribute fingerpaint paper and paints to the children. Have them write *i* on their papers and then write one word that begins with that letter and sound. Read the words aloud.

**Second-Language Support**
To give non-native English speakers additional support, you might wish to hold up illustrations for unfamiliar words as you give clues about them or use them in sentences.

# Initial Consonants Review: /k/*k*, /r/*r*, /s/*s*, /v/*v*

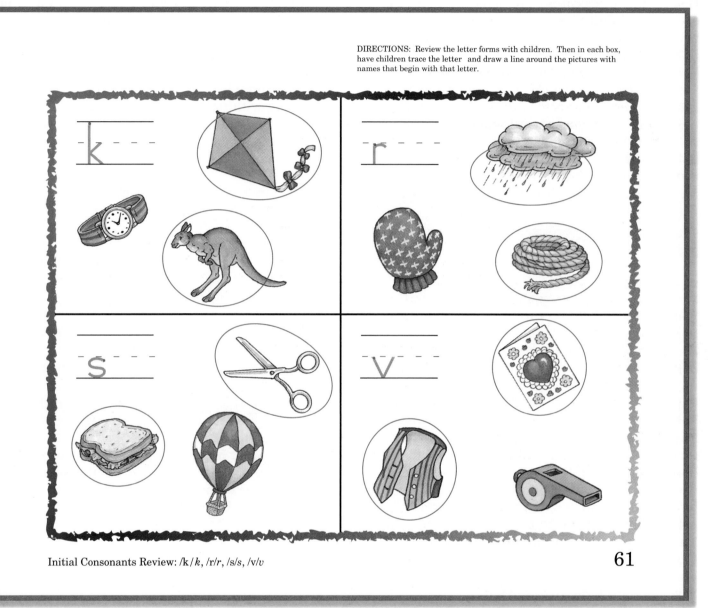

DIRECTIONS: Review the letter forms with children. Then in each box, have children trace the letter and draw a line around the pictures with names that begin with that letter.

Initial Consonants Review: /k/*k*, /r/*r*, /s/*s*, /v/*v*

61

## OBJECTIVES

Phonics and Decoding Skills

Recognize initial consonants: /k/*k*, /r/*r*, /s/*s*, /v/*v*

Recognize final consonants: /k/*k*, /r/*r*, /s/*s*

## MATERIALS

ABC cards or letter cards for *Kk, Rr, Ss, Vv*; picture cards for words beginning with *k, r, s, v*; **Sing a Sound Audiocassette**, Tape 3

- Place the letter cards *K, k, R, r, S, s, V,* and *v* on the chalkboard ledge. Ask children to identify the letters as lowercase or capital.
- Place picture cards for *kangaroo, rug, seal,* and *violin* on the chalkboard ledge. Ask children to name each object and say the beginning sound. Then ask children to name the letter that stands for the beginning sound in *kangaroo.* Call on a volunteer to place the kangaroo beside the letter *k.* Continue matching pictures and letters in this manner.

## DEVELOP/APPLY

### Use the Page
- Write the number 61 on the chalkboard and say it aloud. Have children turn to page 61 in their books.
- Direct children's attention to the first box on the left top of the page. Point to the letter and have children identify it as *k.* Tell children to write over the letter, starting at the red dot. You may wish to model how to form the letter on the chalkboard. Then point to the pictures in the box and have children identify them. Ask children to name the pictures whose names begin with /k/*k* and then to draw a line around the pictures.
- In the box to the right, have children identify and write over the letter *r* and then draw a line around the pictures whose names begin with /r/*r.* Continue this procedure with *s* and *v.*

### Writing
Make a picture graph on the bulletin board. Hand out toy advertisements in newspaper circulars or catalogs. Divide the class into four groups for each key letter and sound: /k/*k,* /r/*r,* /s/*s,* or /v/*v.* Have children cut out the pictures, glue them on the graph under the appropriate letter, and then label each item. Read the completed graph together. Decide which letter was used to name the most toys.

- Divide the class into two equal teams for an "Over, Under Relay." First, collect picture cards for words beginning with the letters *k, r, s,* and *v.* Have members of each team stand in a line, one behind the other. At a prearranged signal, hand a picture card to the first person in each line. Instruct children to hand the card to the person behind them. The first person should pass the card over his or her head, the second person passes under his or her legs, the third person passes over, and so on. When the card reaches the last person in line, the child identifies the letter and the name of the picture that begins with that letter. The child then walks with the card in hand to the front of the line. The teacher exchanges the old card for a new one and the relay continues. The first team to get back to their original lineup wins.
- Write these consonants on the chalkboard and have them identified: *k, r, s, v.* Then read aloud favorite nursery rhymes and have children stamp their feet when they hear an initial sound: /k/, /r/, /s/, /v/.
- Place the **Sing a Sound Audiocassette** for this unit in a listening center. Encourage children to sing the songs again, listening for the key sounds and enjoying the music.

**ACTIVITIES** **CHALLENGE**

**Final Consonants:** /k/*k,* /r/*r,* /s/*s*
Display the letter cards *k, r, s,* and draw three adjoining boxes on the chalkboard. Show the letter card for *k* and say the word *Jack.* Have children tell whether they hear the /k/*k* at the beginning or at the end of the word. Have a volunteer write the letter *k* in the last box on the chalkboard. Continue this procedure, having children write the designated letter in the box to show the position of the letter in the word. You may wish to use these words: *rock, jar, sick, gas, bus.*

# Listening, Speaking, Viewing

62

Listening, Speaking, Viewing

Macmillan/McGraw-Hill

## OBJECTIVES

Listening, Speaking, Viewing Skills

Apply Comprehension Strategies in Viewing Activities

Compare and contrast

Identify sequence

## MATERIALS

*Zoo-Be-Doo* Little Books, coated wire lengths or pipe cleaners, letter cards *Qq, Ww, Yy, Zz,* and *Uu*

- Distribute individual books of *Zoo-Be-Doo*. Write the letters *Zz* on the chalkboard and have children flip through their books looking for words that begin with capital or lowercase *Zz* (*Zoo, zoo, zebra, zookeeper*). Write the *Z* words on the chalkboard and read them aloud with children.
- Have children compare the picture of the zebra to pictures of the yak, quail, and walrus in their Little Books. Ask children to compare each animal to the zebra and decide which one is most like the zebra. Children may decide that the yak is most like the zebra because it has four legs, is a large mammal, has hair and a thin tail, and lives on land.

## DEVELOP/APPLY

### Use the Page

- Write the number 62 on the chalkboard and say it aloud. Have children turn to page 62 in their books.
- Invite children to tell a story about the outdoor art class by asking these questions: *What animals are being molded from clay? Some children are making a walrus. What materials are they using? What are the children under the umbrella making? How do you think the children got the idea to make these animals?*
- Draw children's attention to the different children in the picture who are making papier-mâché zebras. Discuss how to make a papier-mâché zebra with the children. First, make a wire outline of the zebra. Next, wrap papier-mâché strips around the wire frame; lastly, paint the model.

### Writing

Have children work in pairs to write or draw pictures of directions for doing a favorite art project. Remind them to discuss with their partner what to do first, next, and last before they write. You may wish to advise writers to list the steps using the numbers 1, 2, 3.

- Display the letter cards *Qq, Ww, Yy, Zz, Uu.* Invite children to bend, twist, and loop pipe cleaners to form the letters.
- Children may enjoy creating sculptures with pipe cleaners. Encourage them to look through magazines and books for pictures of their favorite zoo animals. Have them use the pictures as models for creating the sculptures. Encourage children to compare their work to the picture.
- Play a game called "Animal Sounds." Have children walk around the room. Call out the name of a zoo animal, and have children act like that animal and make the appropriate sounds for that animal. When you say "Walk," children quietly walk around the room until you call out another animal's name.

### MEETING INDIVIDUAL NEEDS

**Second-Language Support**
Non-native English speakers may have difficulty understanding the term *sculpture*. Explain that a sculpture is a figure or statue that is made of wood, wire, clay, or other art materials. If possible, display some real sculptures or show pictures of different sculptures.

# Letter Identification: *Q, W, Y, Z, U*

DIRECTIONS: Have children point to each colored circle as you name it and then draw a line around the letter you name: yellow circle, *Q*; red circle, *W*; blue circle, *Y* ; green circle, *Z*; orange circle, *U*.

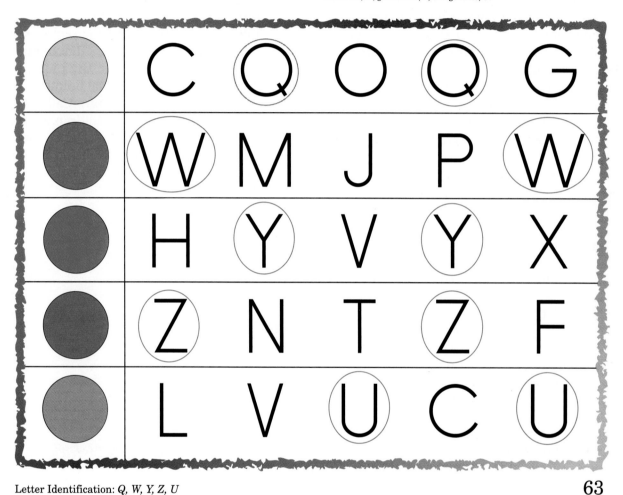

Letter Identification: *Q, W, Y, Z, U*

63

## OBJECTIVES

Phonics and Decoding Skills

Identify capital letters: *Q, W, Y, Z, U*

## MATERIALS

ABC cards or letter cards for *Q, W, Y, Z, U;* alphabet chart; newspapers; markers; boxes; beanbags

## ACTIVITIES

# BUILD BACKGROUND

- Tell children that today they will be learning the names of five more capital letters. Display the individual letter cards for *Q, W, Y, Z,* and *U* and an alphabet chart. Begin the lesson by having children match each letter, without naming it, to the same letter on the chart.
- Sing "The Alphabet Song" with the children. As you come to the letters *Q, W, Y, Z,* and *U,* stop and point to that letter on the letter cards or on the alphabet chart.
- Distribute the letter cards *Q, W, Y, Z,* and *U,* one to each child. Write one of the letters on the chalkboard. Ask children who are holding the same letter card to stand and show their letter. Then have the children say the name of the letter aloud before writing the letter on the chalkboard.

# DEVELOP/APPLY

### Use the Page
- Write the number 63 on the chalkboard and say it aloud. Have children turn to page 63 in their books.
- Have children find and point to the yellow circle in the first row. Invite them to name the letters they know. Then ask a volunteer to name the letter in the first row that has a line around it. Have children draw a line around each capital *Q.*
- Next, ask children to point to the red circle in the second row and name the letters they know. Then have them draw a line around each capital *W.*
- In the row with the blue circle, have children name the letters they know and draw a line around each capital *Y.*
- Continue in this way with the two remaining rows for capital letters *Z* and *U.*

### Reading
Invite children to look at sections of the newspaper for the letters *Q, W, Y, Z,* and *U.* Have children highlight those letters with yellow marker.

## ACTIVITIES

# REINFORCE

- Place letter cards for *Q, W, Y, Z,* and *U* on the chalkboard ledge. Let children play tic-tac-toe at the chalkboard. Ask pairs of children to choose two letters from those displayed to play the game. If children are not familiar with the game, briefly explain how to play.
- Play a game of "Musical Chairs" with the children. Place a letter card (*Q, W, Y, Z,* or *U*) on each chair. Have children march around the chairs to music. When the music stops, each child is to pick up the card on the chair closest to him or her, sit down, and identify the letter.
- Set up five boxes. Label the boxes, each with a capital letter *Q, W, Y, Z,* or *U.* Have children, in turn, stand at a throw line and toss a beanbag into the appropriate box when you name a letter.

## MEETING INDIVIDUAL NEEDS

**Second-Language Support**
Some children may have difficulty discriminating between capital *Z* and capital *S.* Have them work in pairs to practice tracing letter cards for the two letters. Encourage children to talk about the differences.

## Letter Identification: *q, w, y, z, u*

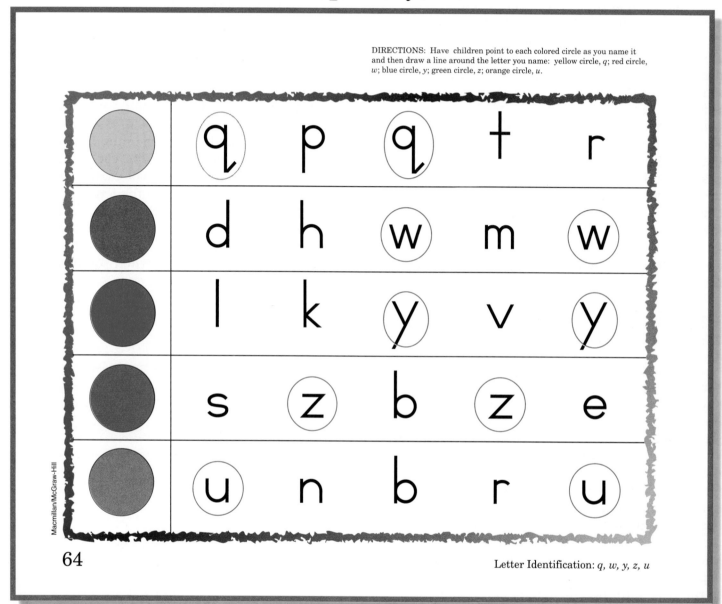

DIRECTIONS: Have children point to each colored circle as you name it and then draw a line around the letter you name: yellow circle, *q*; red circle, *w*; blue circle, *y*; green circle, *z*; orange circle, *u*.

Macmillan/McGraw-Hill

64

Letter Identification: *q, w, y, z, u*

## OBJECTIVES

Phonics and Decoding Skills

Identify lowercase letters: *q, w, y, z, u*

## MATERIALS

ABC cards or letter cards for *Q, q, W, w, Y, y, Z, z,* and *U, u;* chart paper; computer or typewriter

## BUILD BACKGROUND

- Display capital letter cards *Q, W, Y, Z, U,* and have them identified. Tell children that today they will be learning about lowercase letters *q, w, y, z,* and *u.*
- Distribute the individual letter cards for *q, w, y, z,* and *u* to each child. Write one of the letters on the chalkboard. Ask children who are holding the same letter card to stand and show their letter. Ask if anyone knows the name of the letter. Name any unfamiliar letters.
- As a follow-up to the activity above, have children with matching letters stand in a group together. Spark interest for letter formation and recognition by inviting children to use their bodies to create the letter. Switch letters and have the groups repeat the activity.

## DEVELOP/APPLY

### Use the Page
- Write the number 64 on the chalkboard and say it aloud. Have children turn to page 64 in their books.
- Have children find and point to the yellow circle in the first row. Invite them to name the letters they know. Then ask a volunteer to name the letter in the first row that has a line around it (lowercase *q*). Have children draw a line around the other lowercase *q* in the row.
- Next, ask children to point to the red circle in the second row and name the letters they know. Then have them draw a line around each lowercase *w.*
- In the row with the blue circle, have children name the letters they know and then draw a line around each lowercase *y.*
- Continue in this way with the two remaining rows for lowercase letters *z* and *u.*

## REINFORCE

- Write the words to the nursery rhyme "Two Little Kittens" on chart paper. Invite children to join in as you say the rhyme aloud. Then call on volunteers to find lowercase letters *q, w, y, z, u* in the rhyme and draw a line around each one.

### Two Little Kittens

Two little kittens
One drizzly night
Began to quarrel
And then to fight,
One had a bone
And the other had none,
And this is the way
The quarrel began.

Review the circled letters with the children. Point out the position of the letters in the words.

- Have children work in pairs to find these letters on classroom materials or bulletin boards. Give each pair of children a set of letter cards for *q, w, y, z,* and *u.* Instruct them to walk around the room, and place their card beside the word with the matching letter. Encourage children to identify the letters.
- Invite children to practice typing the letters *q, w, y, z,* and *u* on a typewriter or computer. Ask children to share their work with the class, naming each letter as they point to it.

# Auditory Discrimination: /kw/*qu*

DIRECTIONS: Help children identify the key picture at the top of the page. Then have them draw a line around the pictures that begin with the same sound as the word *quilt*. Have children think of other words that begin with the same sound as *quilt*.

Auditory Discrimination: /kw/*qu*    Children should also circle quilt, quarter, question mark.                    65

## OBJECTIVES

Phonics and Decoding Skills

Discrimination among initial sounds

## MATERIALS

Picture or illustration of a quilt or a real quilt, drawing paper, objects or pictures of objects whose names begin with /kw/*qu*, card with question mark

- Show a picture of a quilt or display a real quilt and have it identified. Explain that a quilt is a blanket or bedspread that has a decorative top layer and a plain bottom layer, and is filled with thick, warm material, such as cotton. Point out the pattern on the displayed quilt and tell children that most quilts have a pattern.
- Say the words *quilt* and *quick* aloud. Ask if the words begin with the same sound. Then say the word *bed* and ask if it begins like *quilt*.
- Have children pretend to pull a quilt up to their chins when they hear a word that begins with the same sound as *quilt*. You may wish to use these words: *quack, quake, quail, cart, seat, quarrel, quart, work, turkey, quarter, queen, pillow, camel, quicksand*.

## DEVELOP/APPLY

### Use the Page

- Write the number 65 on the chalkboard and say it aloud. Have children turn to page 65 in their books.
- Point to the key picture at the top of the page and have it identified as a quilt. Invite children to describe what is happening in the picture. You may wish to prompt children with these questions: *What is the girl doing in the meadow? What did one baby bird find? Does he know what it is? What makes you think so?* Encourage children to identify the different things they see in the picture.
- Then point to the queen in the picture. Encourage children to tell why a line has been drawn around her. Explain that the word *queen* begins with the same sound as *quilt*. Have children say the words *quilt* and *queen* and then trace over the line using their pencils.
- Encourage children to complete the page by drawing a line around each object whose name begins with the same sound as *quilt*. Have children think of other words beginning with the same sound as *quilt*.

- Display a card with a question mark and identify it. Explain that this mark is used at the end of a question. Point out that a question asks something such as: *Does the queen wear a crown?*
- Next give each child a sheet of drawing paper and have children draw a question mark. Tell them that you are going to ask some questions. Have them hold up their question marks each time they hear a word that begins with the same sound as *quilt*. Remind children to also hold up their question marks to mark the end of the question. Use these questions:

  *Did the quails quarrel?*
  *Will a quarter buy a quart of milk?*
  *Can a queen quack?*
  *Can you pull the quail from the quicksand?*
  *Where is the quiet queen?*
  *How many quilts does the queen need?*

- Have children complete each group of words by adding a word that belongs with the group and begins with /kw/*qu*.

  | | |
  |---|---|
  | penny, nickel, dime | *(quarter)* |
  | robin, turkey, bluebird | *(quail)* |
  | moo, meow, bark | *(quack)* |
  | fuss, argue, fight | *(quarrel)* |
  | king, prince, princess | *(queen)* |

# Initial Consonant: /kw/*qu*

DIRECTIONS: Help children identify the letters and pictures. Ask them to draw a line around the letter *q* in the word *quilt* and write *q* on the lines. Then in each box, have children write the letter *q* above each picture that begins with the same letter and sound as the key picture.

quilt

q   q

1. _____
q
quarter

2. _____
bird

3. _____
q
queen

4. _____
airplane

5. _____
car

6. _____
q
?
question mark

7. _____
cat

8. _____
q
quack
quack

Macmillan/McGraw-Hill

66

## OBJECTIVES

Phonics and Decoding Skills

Recognize initial consonant: /kw/*qu*

## MATERIALS

ABC cards or letter cards for *Q* and *q*, picture cards, jump ropes

- Display a picture or illustration of a yellow sun and have children identify it. Then invite children to tell why the sun is important to us. (It gives off light and heat. It helps plants to grow, and plants provide food for animals and people.)
- Have children listen as you say the words *yellow* and *yo-yo*. Ask if the two words begin with the same sound. Have children say the words aloud. Then say the words *yellow* and *wagon*, and ask if the words begin with the same sound.
- Tell children to stand up. Have them bend down and curl up into a ball. Tell them you are going to say some words. Explain that when they hear you say a word that begins with the same sound as *yellow*, they should rise and stretch out their hands as if they were a big, yellow sun rising in the sky. (Demonstrate for children.) Explain if they hear a word that begins with a different sound, they should stay crouched as if they were a sun setting. Say these words: *yam, yesterday, girl, you, very, house, yogurt, yo-yo.*

## DEVELOP/APPLY

**Use the Page**

- Write the number 69 on the chalkboard. Have children turn to page 69 in their books.
- Direct children's attention to the key picture at the top of the page and have it identified. Then help children identify the animals and objects in the big picture. Invite children to tell a story about the picture.
- Have children point to the yardstick in the picture. Explain that a yardstick is used to measure how long or how tall things are. Then ask why there is a line drawn around it. (*Yardstick* begins with the same sound as the key picture, *yellow*.) Have children say *yellow* and *yardstick* and trace over the line with a pencil.
- Have children complete the page by drawing a line around each object whose name begins with the same sound as *yellow*. Then encourage children to think of other words that begin with the same sound as *yellow*.

## REINFORCE

- Ask volunteers to complete this sentence: "Yesterday I saw a yellow _____." Tell children to think of something they might see that begins with the same sound as *yesterday* and *yellow*.
- Distribute letter cards for *Y* and *y*. Tell children you are going to say some word pairs. Have them hold up their letter cards when they hear a word pair that begins with the same sound as *yellow*. Use these word pairs: *yellow, yawn; yellow, yes; yellow, water; yellow, yak; yellow, very; yellow, yet.*
- Tell children that you are going to say some sentences. After you say a sentence, have them repeat the words in the sentence that begin with the same sound as *yellow*. Use these sentences:

  **1.** The baby thought the egg yolk was yummy!
  **2.** Ying has a blue yo-yo.
  **3.** Yesterday, the baby yelled loudly.
  **4.** I like to eat yogurt and yams.
  **5.** Look at the yellow butterfly in the yard!

- To reinforce the /y/ sound, play the traditional song "Yankee Doodle" (**Sing a Sound Audiocassette**, Tape 3, Side 2). Have children clap every time they hear the word *Yankee*.

# Initial Consonant: /y/y

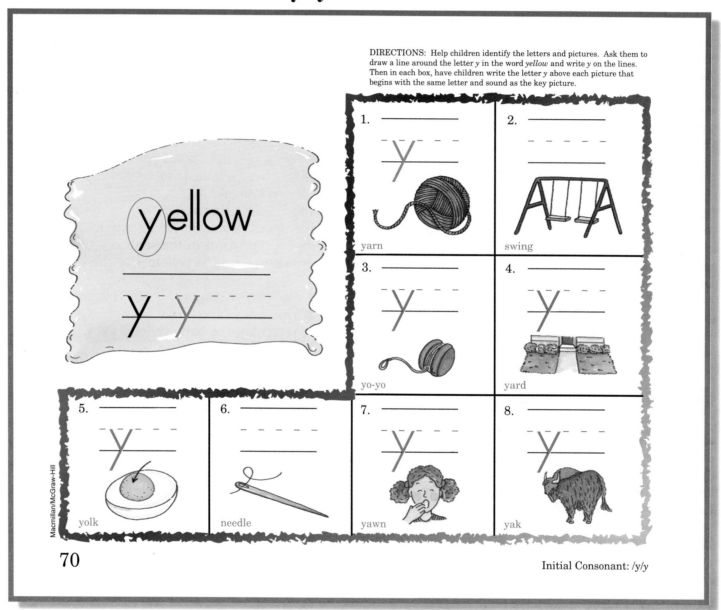

DIRECTIONS: Help children identify the letters and pictures. Ask them to draw a line around the letter y in the word *yellow* and write y on the lines. Then in each box, have children write the letter y above each picture that begins with the same letter and sound as the key picture.

yellow

y y

1. Y — yarn

2. swing

3. Y — yo-yo

4. y — yard

5. Y — yolk

6. needle

7. y — yawn

8. y — yak

Macmillan/McGraw-Hill

70

Initial Consonant: /y/y

## OBJECTIVES

Phonics and Decoding Skills

Recognize initial consonant: /y/y

## MATERIALS

ABC cards or letter cards for *Y* and *y*, yellow crayons, drawing paper, chart paper, picture cards whose names begin with /y/*y* and other consonants

- Display the letter cards *Y* and *y*. As you point to each letter, encourage volunteers to identify each as capital *Y* or lowercase *y*. Write the word *yellow* on the chalkboard and point to the letter *y*.
- Ask children if the word *yawn* begins like *yellow*. Then have children pretend to yawn each time they hear a word that begins like *yellow* or *yawn*. Use these words: *yak, little, your, you, just, yogurt, vest, yell*.

## DEVELOP/APPLY

### Use the Page
- Write the number 70 on the chalkboard and say it aloud. Have children turn to page 70 in their books.
- Direct children's attention to the key picture and have it identified. Ask children to name the letter at the beginning of the word *yellow*, and then draw a line around the letter *y*.
- Point to the letter *y* on the lines in the yellow splash. Have children identify the *y*. Invite them to write over the letter, starting at the red dot. You may wish to form the letter on the chalkboard. Then have children practice writing the letter *y*.
- Ask children to point to the picture of the ball of yarn. Have them say *yellow* and *yarn*. Ask if the two words begin with the same letter and sound. Then point out the letter *y* above the yarn and have children write over the letter.
- Point out the remaining boxes and ask children to identify the picture in each one. Explain that they will write *y* above each picture that begins with the same sound and letter as *yellow*.

### Writing
On the chalkboard, write the *y* words children find in the classroom. Then ask them to choose a word and use it in a sentence. Have them write their sentence in their Journals.

- Give each child a yellow crayon and drawing paper. Have children write *y* at the top of their papers; then ask them to draw something that could be yellow. Call on volunteers to show and tell about their pictures.
- Display picture cards of objects that begin with /y/y and other consonants along the chalkboard ledge. Call on volunteers to choose a picture whose name begins with the same sound and letter as *yellow*, and then make up a sentence about it. Write children's sentences on the chalkboard, and have them underline each word that begins with the same sound and letter as *yellow*.
- Draw a large yellow daffodil on chart paper. Have children, in turn, write a word on each petal of the daffodil that begins with /y/y. Read the completed list with the children.

# Auditory Discrimination: /z/z

DIRECTIONS: Help children identify the key picture at the top of the page. Then have them draw a line around the pictures that begin with the same sound as the word *zero*. Have children think of other words that begin with the same sound as *zero*.

Auditory Discrimination: /z/z    Children should also circle zebras, zipper, zoo.    71

## OBJECTIVES

Phonics and Decoding Skills

Discriminate among initial sounds

Discriminate among final sounds

## MATERIALS

Illustration of the numeral zero, **Sing a Sound Audiocassette**, Tape 3

- Display a numeral card for 0, or write a large 0 on the chalkboard. Identify the numeral with the children. Then write the numerals 0–10 on the chalkboard and have children count aloud. Explain that each number can also be written as a word.
- Have children listen as you say the words *zero* and *zoo*. Ask if the two words begin with the same sound. Have children say the words aloud. Then say the words *zero* and *yellow*, and ask if the words begin with the same sound.
- Tell children you are going to say some words. Explain that when they hear you say a word that begins with the same sound as *zero*, they should raise their right hand. Say these words: *zoo, post, zebra, zinnia, water, yak, zipper, zany, kiss.*

## DEVELOP/APPLY

**Use the Page**
- Write the number 71 on the chalkboard and say it aloud. Have children turn to page 71 in their books.
- Direct children's attention to the key picture at the top of the page and have it identified. Then help children to identify the animals in the picture. Invite children to tell a story about the picture.
- Have children point to the zigzag in the picture. Ask why there is a line drawn around it. (*Zigzag* begins with the same sound as the key picture.) Have children say *zero* and *zigzag* and trace over the line with a pencil.
- Have children complete the page by drawing a line around each object whose name begins with the same sound as *zero*. Then encourage children to think of other words that begin with the same sound as *zero*.

- Teach this rhyme to the children:

  We're going to the zoo.
  We're going to the zoo.
  You can come, too.
  We're going to the zoo.

  After children have learned the rhyme, ask them to identify the word that begins with the same sound as *zero*. Have children march around the room as they recite.

- Tell children you are going to say some word pairs. Have them make a zero with their thumb and forefinger each time both words in the pair begin with the same sound as *zero*. Use these word pairs: *zero, zip; zero, yarn; zero, zipper; zero, sail; zero, party; zero, zest.*
- Tell children you are going to say some sentences. After you say a sentence, have them repeat the words in the sentence that begin with the same sound as *zero*. Use these sentences:

  **1.** Zeke is a zany zebra.
  **2.** Zippy likes the number zero.
  **3.** Zelda zigzags around the room.
  **4.** Can you zip up my zipper?

- As an added activity, play "Going to the Zoo," from the **Sing a Sound Audiocassette**, Tape 3, Side 2. As children become familiar with the song, encourage them to clap their hands each time they sing the word *zoo.*

### CHALLENGE

**Final Consonant:** /z/z
As you say the following words, have children repeat each one after you: *buzz, fuzz, jazz, quiz.* Ask how the words are alike. Help children to recognize that all the words end with /z/.

# Initial Consonant: /z/z

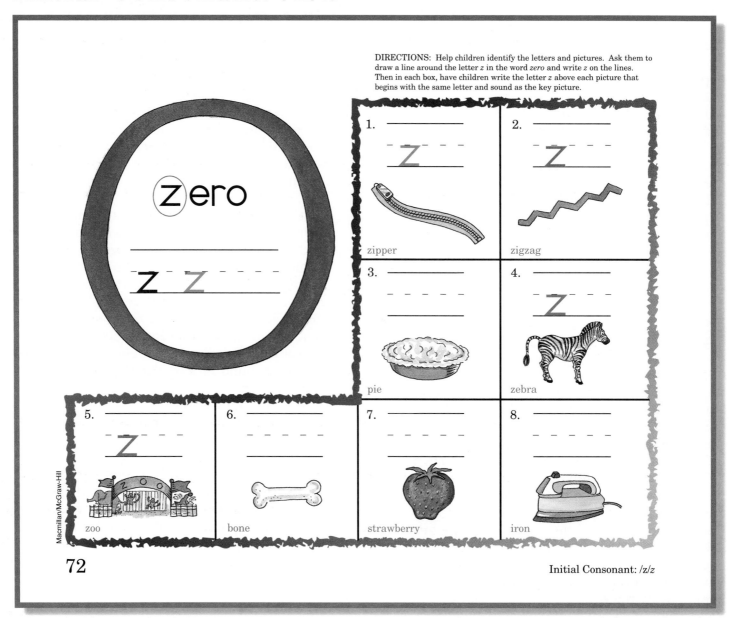

DIRECTIONS: Help children identify the letters and pictures. Ask them to draw a line around the letter *z* in the word *zero* and write *z* on the lines. Then in each box, have children write the letter *z* above each picture that begins with the same letter and sound as the key picture.

zero

z z

1. z — zipper

2. z — zigzag

3. — pie

4. z — zebra

5. z — zoo

6. — bone

7. — strawberry

8. — iron

Macmillan/McGraw-Hill

72

Initial Consonant: /z/z

## OBJECTIVES

Phonics and Decoding Skills

Recognize initial consonant: /z/z

Recognize final consonant: /z/z

## MATERIALS

ABC cards or letter cards for *Z* and *z*, *Zoo-Be-Doo*, sandpaper, drawing paper, crayons, chart paper

- Display the letter cards for *Z* and *z*. As you point to each letter in turn, encourage volunteers to identify it as capital *Z* or lowercase *z*. Write the word *zero* on the chalkboard and have children say it with you. Elicit that the word *zero* begins with the letter *z*.
- Ask children to clap their hands when they hear you say a word that begins with the same letter and sound as *zero*. Use these words: *yak, zip, zone, soap, zoo, pail, zany.*

## DEVELOP/APPLY

### Use the Page
- Write the number 72 on the chalkboard and say it aloud. Have children turn to page 72 in their books.
- Direct children's attention to the key picture and have it identified. Have children point to the word *zero* and say it aloud. Then ask children to name the letter at the beginning of the word *zero* and draw a line around it.
- Point to the letter *z* on the lines in the zero. Have children identify the lowercase *z*. Invite them to write over the letter, starting at the red dot. You may wish to form the letter on the chalkboard. Then have children practice writing the letter *z*.
- Ask children to point to the picture of the zipper. Have them say *zero* and *zipper.* Ask if the two words begin with the same letter and sound. Then point out the letter *z* above the zipper, and have children write over the letter.
- Point out the remaining boxes and ask children to identify the picture in each one. Explain that they will write *z* above each picture that begins with the same letter and sound as *zero*.

### Reading
Invite children to look through *Zoo-Be-Doo* and find words that begin with the same letter and sound as *zero.*

- Cut out the letter *z* from sandpaper, and give each pair of children a letter, a sheet of drawing paper, and crayons. Have partners take turns tracing over the sandpaper letter several times to make a *z* design.
- Brainstorm some *z* words with the children and write them on the chalkboard. Then, begin a story about Zeke the Zebra and write it on chart paper. Call on volunteers to add a sentence to the story. Remind children to use words that begin with the same sound and letter as *zero* in their sentences. Write the children's sentences on chart paper. When the story has been completed, read it with the children. Ask volunteers to draw a line around each word that begins with the same letter and sound as *zero.*
- Play "I'm Thinking Of . . ." with the children. Begin by saying "I'm thinking of an animal that has black and white stripes. What is it?" (zebra) Continue the game by giving clues for *zipper, zero,* and *zoo.*

**Final Consonant:** /z/z
Ask children to identify where they hear the /z/ sound in each of these words: *jazz, buzz, quiz.* Write the words on the chalkboard and underline the *z*'s in each word. Remind children that some words can begin with /z/z and some words can end with /z/z.

# Auditory Discrimination: /u/*u*

DIRECTIONS: Help children identify the key picture at the top of the page. Then have them draw a line around the pictures that begin with the same sound as the word *umbrella*. Have children think of other words that begin with the same sound as *umbrella*.

Auditory Discrimination: /u/*u*    Children should also circle udder, up, upon.

73

## OBJECTIVES

Phonics and Decoding Skills

Discriminate among initial sounds

## MATERIALS

Picture or illustration of an umbrella, ABC cards or letter cards for *U* and *u*, pictures of objects whose names begin with /u/*u* and other consonants

## BUILD BACKGROUND

- Display a picture or an illustration of an umbrella, or show a real umbrella. Have it identified. Invite children to tell when they have used an umbrella.
- Have children listen as you say the words *umbrella* and *up*. Ask if the two words begin with the same sound. Have children say the words aloud. Then say the words *umbrella* and *zero,* and ask if the words begin with the same sound.
- Tell children you are going to say some words. Explain that when they hear you say a word that begins with the same sound as *umbrella,* they should pretend to hold an umbrella over their heads. Say these words: *up, under, elephant, unzip, apple, understand, utter, icicle, umpire.*

## DEVELOP/APPLY

### Use the Page
- Write the number 73 on the chalkboard and say it aloud. Have children turn to page 73 in their books.
- Direct children's attention to the key picture at the top of the page and have it identified. Then help children to identify the objects in the picture. Invite children to tell a story about the picture.
- Have children point to the chick under the stool. Ask why there is a line drawn around it. (*Under* begins with the same sound as the key picture.) Have children say *umbrella* and *under* and trace over the line with a pencil.
- Have children complete the page by drawing a line around each object whose name begins with the same sound as *umbrella.* Then encourage children to think of other words that begin with the same sound as *umbrella.*

## REINFORCE

- Place pictures of objects whose names begin with /u/*u* and other vowel or consonant sounds in groups of three on the chalkboard ledge. Have the pictures identified. Then have volunteers find the picture in each group whose name begins with the same sound as *umbrella.*
- Tell children you are going to say some word pairs. Have them point their right thumb up when each word in the pair begins with the same sound as *umbrella.* (You may wish to demonstrate this before beginning the activity.) Use these word pairs: *unfair, pest; up, udder; jump, undo; umpire, uncle; unhappy, until; under, otter.*
- Tell children you are going to say some sentences. After you say a sentence, have them repeat the words in the sentence that begin with the same sound as *umbrella.* Use these sentences:

1. Umberto understands the story.
2. Topsy is sleeping under the umbrella.
3. The umpire tells us to get up!
4. Will Uncle Ed come upstairs?

# Initial Vowel: /u/u

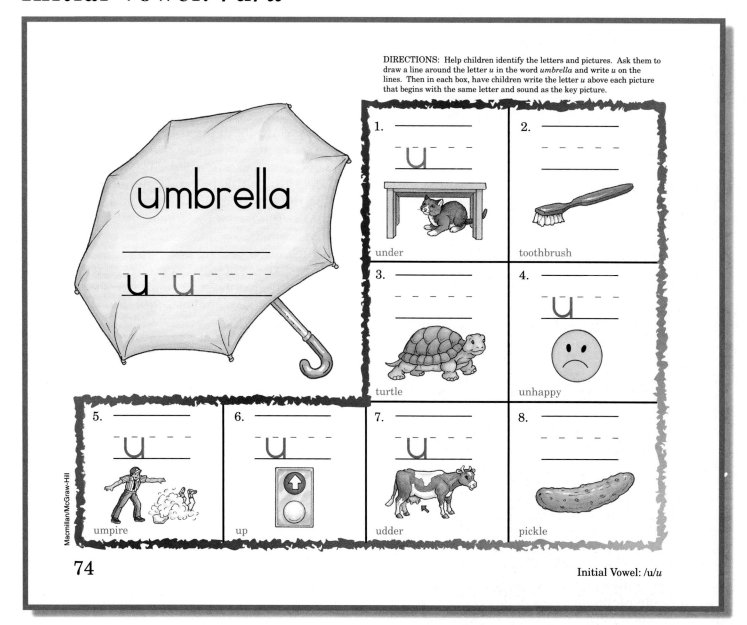

DIRECTIONS: Help children identify the letters and pictures. Ask them to draw a line around the letter *u* in the word *umbrella* and write *u* on the lines. Then in each box, have children write the letter *u* above each picture that begins with the same letter and sound as the key picture.

umbrella

u u

1. under

2. toothbrush

3. turtle

4. unhappy

5. umpire

6. up

7. udder

8. pickle

Macmillan/McGraw-Hill

74

Initial Vowel: /u/u

## OBJECTIVES

Phonics and Decoding Skills

Recognize initial consonant: /u/u

## MATERIALS

ABC cards or letter cards for *U* and *u*, clay, drawing paper, chart paper, crayons, magazines, store flyers, newspapers

- Display the letter cards *U* and *u*. As you point to each letter, encourage volunteers to identify it as capital *U* or lowercase *u*. Write the word *umbrella* on the chalkboard and point to the letter *u*.
- Have children sit down. Ask them to stand up when they hear you say a word that begins with the same sound as *umbrella*. Use these words: *up, vase, under, west, uncle, umpire, exit.*

## DEVELOP/APPLY

### Use the Page
- Write the number 74 on the chalkboard and say it aloud. Have children turn to page 74 in their books.
- Direct children's attention to the key picture and ask children to identify the letter at the beginning of the word *umbrella* and then draw a line around the letter *u*.
- Point to the letter *u* on the lines in the umbrella. Have children identify the lowercase *u*. Invite them to write over the letter, starting at the red dot. You may wish to form the letter on the chalkboard. Then have children practice writing the letter *u*.
- Ask children to point to the picture of the cat under the table. Have them say *umbrella* and *under*. Ask if the two words begin with the same letter and sound. Then point out the letter *u* above the table and have children write over the letter.
- Point out the remaining boxes and ask children to identify the picture in each one. Explain that they will write *u* above each picture that begins with the same sound and letter as *umbrella*.

### Writing
Have children write in their Journals a word that begins with the same sound and letter as *umbrella*.

- Distribute crayons and drawing paper to the children. Have children fold their papers in half vertically. Have children practice writing capital *U* on one side and lowercase *u* on the other side.
- Have children use clay to make a lowercase *u*, and then use their finger to trace the letter.
- Have children look for words that begin with the same sound and letter as *umbrella* in old newspapers, magazines, or store flyers. Have them draw a line around the words they find and then share their words with a classmate.
- Brainstorm some /u/*u* words with the children and write them on the chalkboard. Draw a large umbrella on chart paper. Then ask children, in turn, to write a word on the umbrella that begins with /u/*u*. Read the words on the umbrella with the children.

# Initial Consonants Review: /kw/*qu*, /w/*w*, /y/*y*, /z/*z*

DIRECTIONS: Review the letter forms with children. Then in each box, have children trace the letter and draw a line around the pictures with names that begin with that letter.

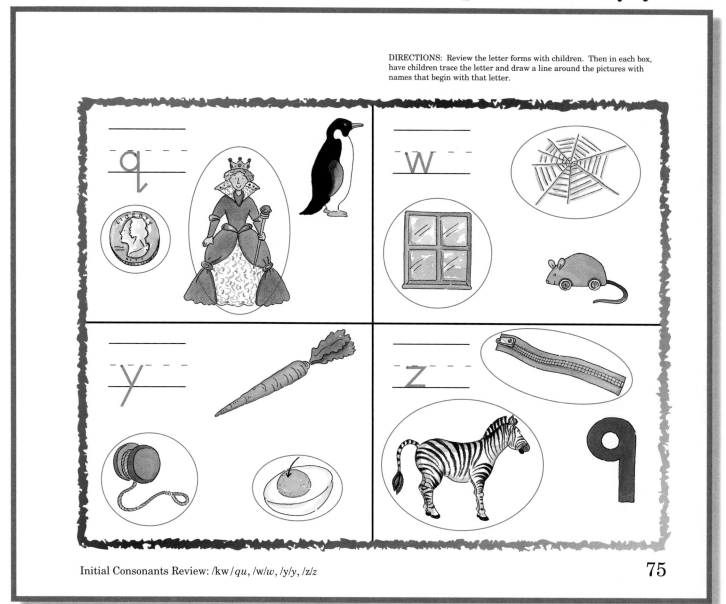

Initial Consonants Review: /kw/*qu*, /w/*w*, /y/*y*, /z/*z*

75

## OBJECTIVES

Phonics and Decoding Skills

Recognize initial consonants:

/kw/*qu*, /w/*w*, /y/*y*, /z/*z*

## MATERIALS

ABC cards or letter cards for *Q, W, Y, Z, q, w, y,* and *z;* picture cards whose names begin with /kw/*qu*, /w/*w*, /y/*y*, /z/*z*; chart paper; magnetic letters; index cards

- Display the letter cards *Q* and *q*. As you point to each letter, encourage volunteers to identify each as capital *Q* or lowercase *q*. Repeat the activity with the other letter cards for *W, w, Y, y,* and *Z, z*.
- Ask children to listen as you say a group of three words. Have them repeat each word group after you and identify the beginning letter and sound. Use these word groups:
  1. queen, quiet, quit
  2. zoo, zone, zebra
  3. west, wind, work
  4. yak, yearn, your
  5. quart, quack, quill
  6. winter, web, will

## DEVELOP/APPLY

### Use the Page
- Write the number 75 on the chalkboard and say it aloud. Have children turn to page 75 in their books.
- Point to the letter *q* on the lines in the first box. Have children identify the lowercase *q*. Invite them to write over the letter, starting at the red dot. You may wish to form the letter on the chalkboard. Then point to the pictures in the box and have them identified. Ask children to draw a line around the pictures whose names begin with /kw/*qu*.
- In the box to the right, have children identify and write over the letter *w*. Then have the pictures in the box identified. Ask children to draw a line around the pictures whose names begin with /w/*w*.
- Continue this procedure with the remaining boxes for the letters *y* and *z*.

### Reading
Have children look for words in their books that begin with *q, w, y,* and *z*.

- Play a game of "Concentration" with the children. Gather three sets of letter cards for *q, w, y, z* and two sets of picture cards for those letters. Mix up the cards and place them face down in rows on a table. Each child then turns over two cards. If one card is a picture card and the other card is a letter card that begins the picture name, the child has a match and removes the cards. If the cards do not match, they are turned over again face down and the next child takes a turn. Remind children to try to remember where the cards are so they can make a match. The child that has the most matches wins the game.
- Display a set of magnetic letters. Challenge volunteers to make up words that begin with *q, w, y,* and *z*. Have other children read the words.
- Make a word wall. Tape a large sheet of butcher paper or chart paper on a wall. Assign each child a letter: *q, w, y,* or *z*. Have children, in turn, write a word on an index card that begins with their assigned letter and tack it to the word wall.

# PICTURE CARDS
## Blackline Masters

Pages 76–82 contain blackline masters for your use in creating picture cards. The objects depicted include those suggested for use in the activities described in this book. To make picture cards, duplicate the pictures, cut them out, and glue them to blank 4" x 6" index cards or pieces of oaktag. Write the corresponding initial consonant on the back of each card. Before using the picture cards, review them with children.

boy

bear

ball

car

cow

cat

dog

donkey

door

fan
feather
fish

girl
goat
game

harp
hat
house

jeep
jar
jet

kite

key

kangaroo

lamp

lion

lock

map

mouse

mask

nest

newspaper

nuts

pig
pan
pencil

queen
quarter
quail

rug
rabbit
refrigerator

seal
sandwich
sock

tiger

table

turkey

vase

violin

van

window

wagon

watch

yarn

yo-yo

yak

zebra
zero
zipper

  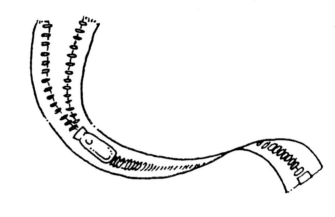

apple
ant
alligator

elephant
elevator
elf

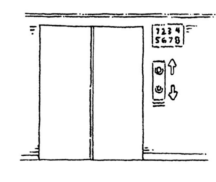 

igloo
insects
inner tube

  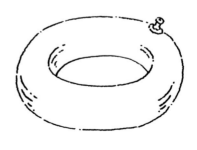

octopus

ox

olive

umpire

umbrella

up